Indoor Grilling

50 Recipes for Electric Grills,
Stovetop Grills, and Smokers

Indoor Grilling

Dwayne Ridgaway

This edition published in 2010 by CRESTLINE
A division of BOOK SALES, INC.
276 Fifth Avenue Suite 206
New York, New York 10001
USA

First published in the United States of America by
Quarry Books, a member of
Quayside Publishing Group
33 Commercial Street
Gloucester, Massachusetts 01930-5089
Telephone: (978) 282-9590
Fax: (978) 283-2742
www.rockpub.com

Library of Congress Cataloging-in-Publication Data
Ridgaway, Dwayne.
    Indoor grilling : 50 recipes for electric grills, stovetop grills, and
smokers/Dwayne Ridgaway.
        p.   cm.
    1. Barbecue cookery. I. Title.
    TX840.B3R55 2005
    641.7'6—dc22   2005007166
                                                               CIP

ISBN-13: 978-0-7858-2635-4
ISBN-10: 0-7858-2635-1

Design: Wilson Harvey, London
Cover Image and Photography: Allan Penn Photography

Printed in China

While working on this project, my family lost an important member—my Uncle George. It is with great love and admiration that I dedicate this book to him.

Introduction
The benefits of indoor grilling and smoking 9

Contents

Introduction

For years, grilling has been one of my favorite cooking techniques, probably because a majority of my childhood memories involve camping and outdoor cooking. Though wonderfully versatile and very easy to master, outdoor grilling does require specialized equipment and the room to store it. It is also most comfortably done in warm weather! For home cooks who are limited by equipment, space, or temperature, or for those who simply want to learn a new cooking technique, I present indoor grilling and smoking.

Though indoor grilling and smoking is not new, it is getting a lot of attention. In fact, the marketplace has already become somewhat saturated with several types of indoor grilling appliances, including electric, built-in, and simple grill pans. It seems there's an indoor grilling pan to fit everyone's comfort level. Not as familiar and most definitely not as abundant are indoor smoking vessels. This piece of equipment, which is basically a glorified roasting pan, allows you to bring the wonderful technique of hardwood smoking inside the comfort of your home, 365 days a year.

As I mentioned before, indoor grilling is not necessarily a new idea, but it is one that may seem a bit mundane. During my research, many of the indoor grilling recipes I found focus heavily on the health aspects while leaving taste and appearance as an afterthought. I have chosen the opposite approach: the delicious dishes found in this book are healthy by nature due to their preparation and cooking methods. Simply put, my recipes are healthy as well as delicious and appealing, and they push the envelope in terms of flavor and ingredient combinations.

In addition to the recipes, this book also contains product reviews and information on a number of grilling and smoking appliances, pans, and utensils. I will guide you through the preparation, use, and care of your equipment and offer my opinion on particular brands.

And last, but not least, this book contains a collection of thoughts and tips that are not only instructional but also designed to inspire you in your own cooking. Whether you complete a recipe exactly as is or tailor it to fit your own preferences, I encourage creative cooking and experimenting in the kitchen.

If you enjoy this book, please look for my other three books: *Lasagna: The Art of Layered Cooking; Pizza: 50 Traditional and Alternative Recipes for the Oven and Grill;* and *Sandwiches, Panini, and Wraps: Recipes for the Original "Anytime, Anywhere" Meal.*

chapter 1

Cooking Techniques: Times, Preparations, and Product Reviews

Cooking Techniques

Indoor grilling offers a simple year-round technique for enjoying the same caramelized flavors and seared characteristics of outdoor grilling right in your own kitchen. Rain or shine, indoor grilling is fun, easy, and quick. Although not complicated, indoor grilling requires some preparation and product knowledge to make sure foods are both cooked through and flavorful.

A thick cut of bone-in meat, such as double-thick pork chops or thick veal chops, makes a beautiful and elegant grilled meal (see page 57). However, when cooking thick cuts of meat it is important to remember to allow the meat to reach its proper internal temperature, as well as to keep in mind what temperatures are necessary for what cuts of meats (see pages 12–13 for actual temperatures). As I mention in the pork and veal recipes, it may be necessary to finish the cooking in the oven to reach the proper internal temperature. Keep in mind that not all electric grilling appliances operate the same way, so cooking times may vary depending on the thickness and the cut of meat.

Cooking vegetables on an indoor grill is a great way to create the robust flavor of grilled vegetables for any meal. Some vegetables, depending on the cut, however, are more tender than others and may not hold up well on an electric grill appliance with a heavy or closing lid.

Marinating meat, fish, or poultry is a great way to impart flavors while also tenderizing the food. But keep this caution in mind: when grilling in cast iron or other steel grill pans, excess marinade or sauce in the pan will probably burn before the actual food is done. In general, use or aim for runny marinades rather than a thick consistency to prevent a big mess in the pan when cooking. The one exception to this is the "mop," which is used with a slow-cooking technique to develop true barbecue flavor. A "mop" is a very thick sauce made with sugars and ingredients that tend to burn quickly at a high temperature, so use a lower temperature for a longer period of time with these recipes.

Indoor smokers are a relatively new introduction. Smoking food is an easy way to impart incredible flavor to just about any type of food. There are a few important things to remember, however, when using an indoor smoker. First, don't overload the wood. It is very easy to think that the amount of wood chips my recipes call for will not be enough to smoke the food. But believe me, it is. Too many wood chips will make your food taste bitter. Second, only use the wood chips intended for the smoker you are using. Generally, indoor smokers require a very finely ground wood product specifically made for stovetop use. Follow the manufacturer's guidelines when it comes to choosing the correct wood chip for the best results.

Lastly, don't be tempted to open the smoker before the full smoking time has elapsed. You will just let out all of the great smoke that had been building, and increase the cooking time required.

Using a spatula on a grill pan is not a good idea, so keep a pair of tongs handy for turning the meat in your pan. Also, don't overcrowd the pan, as this only makes it more difficult to turn or remove the food you're preparing. If you're cooking for a crowd, use two or more grill pans or a large double-sided grill/griddle pan to cook more food all at once. Alternatively, cook your food in batches and keep the cooked foods warm in an oven set to low while you finish the rest.

Knowing the proper internal temperature is key. Meat and poultry must be grilled or cooked to a certain internal temperature to kill any bacteria that may cause food-borne illness. Simply put, the following method is the safest way of ensuring your food is properly done.

To get an accurate internal temperature, you will need a probe-style, instant-read chef's thermometer, available in most kitchen supply stores. Probe thermometers are available in digital read and gauge read. The temperature range is 0°F to 220°F (–18°C to 105°C), providing a wide range of measurements for both cold and hot food. When purchasing an instant-read thermometer, insist on one that can be calibrated: following the manufacturer's instructions for proper use and maintenance will allow you to have accurate temperature readings every time.

Chicken and other poultry should always be cooked to an internal temperature of 165°F (75°C). Pork, on the other hand, should be cooked to an internal temperature of 145°F (65°C). (Even if you like your pork more well done, make sure it reaches an internal temperature of at least 145°F [65°C].)

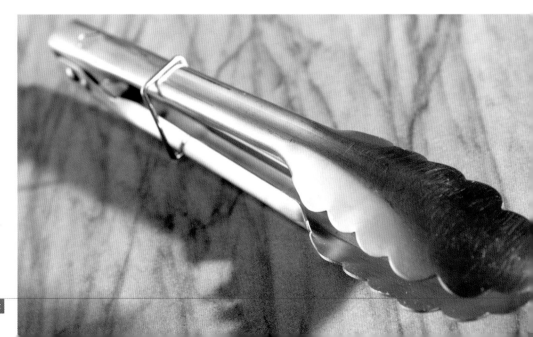

There will always be exceptions to these internal temperature rules, however, depending on the cut of meat, the method of preparation, and personal taste. Suggestions for bending these rules are included in certain recipes, such as in my Grilled Asian Pork Tenderloin with Fried Bananas and Grilled Polenta (page 58).

Some recipes ask that you bind ingredients together with twine. This technique encourages the juices and flavors to meld, as well as simply making the ingredients easy to handle during preparation.

[Preparation]

Short of deciding on the menu and the cooking appliance, there really isn't much preparation needed with indoor grilling. Indoor grills should be used on a hard, flat surface to prevent any burning or injuries. As with any cooking appliance or electrical equipment, never let children handle the hot appliance and don't leave the equipment unattended. When you are done cooking on your electric grill, I suggest unplugging it, cleaning it (following the manufacturer's recommendations), and storing it away from the countertop.

Beef and other meats are typically cooked to different internal temperatures depending on whether you prefer rare, medium, or well done. For rare, the internal temperature should read 120°F (50°C); for medium rare, 125°F (55°C); for medium, 135°F (60°C); and for well done, 145°F (65°C). When grilling steaks and such, be sure to take them off the grill at these temperatures and let them stand for about 5 to 10 minutes before serving. The food will actually continue to cook for a few minutes, and the result is a perfectly done (and juicy) steak.

Choosing a cooking appliance for indoor grilling is just as important as selecting one for outdoor cooking. It's important to put some thought and consideration into purchasing the right appliance or piece of equipment for your level of cooking expertise and/or lifestyle. If you've been in a kitchen or housewares store recently, you may have noticed the vast selection of indoor grilling appliances and equipment (less so for indoor smoking appliances, but there are a few options available). Because there are so many grill choices, I will decipher some of the differences.

First of all, there are big differences between a panini grill, a grill press, a George Foreman grill, and an open grill.

[George Foreman–Style Grills]
With an ever-growing line of products, the George Foreman–style of indoor electric grilling appliances are designed to offer lower fat grill-like cooking. These appliances are designed with their heating surfaces tipped at a slight angle in the front, which allows the food's fat drippings to run off. In theory, this reduces the amount of fat in your meal. These are great appliances: very easy to use and simple to clean up. When using a George Foreman–style appliance, you

Indoor Grilling **and** Smoking Appliances

may have to accommodate the slight angle to the pan to get your desired results. When I cook panini in my Foreman grill, for instance, I prop up the front end to create a level cooking surface. This prevents the ingredients in the panini from melting and running out of the center of the sandwich. The George Foreman appliances range in size and intended use. There are small grills that will accommodate only a single burger or panini, or larger versions for bigger output. My George Foreman grill, for example, cooks about four servings at a time.

[Panini Grills]

Another popular type of grilling appliance is the panini grill. *Panini* (Italian for sandwich) are grilled sandwiches that are cooked on this specific style of grill; such grills feature a pressing top that weighs down the sandwich while it is cooking. These grills are also excellent for grilling other foods because they get very hot; they sear the food; and they produce nice, deep, straight grill marks. Electric panini grills are similar to the George Foreman grills but with two important differences. A typical panini grill is flat and level, with no slant to the cooking surface. In addition, the lid is designed to adjust to the thickness of what is being cooked while at the same time applying pressure to ensure the bottom is grilled as well as the top.

Most panini grills have a light that indicates when the device is preheated and when the cooking is complete. Don't depend solely on the red light to determine when the food is done, however. The indicator light is basically a thermostat designed to indicate when the grill has reached its hottest temperature, not necessarily that the item is done. For this reason, a thick panini or cut of meat may take longer to cook on the inside than what the machine is able to measure on the outside.

I recommend either the George Foreman–style grills or a panini grill for easy indoor grilling. Both styles of appliance are good for cooking almost any dish, including meat, fish, poultry, sandwiches, and vegetables. Of the two, I prefer the level design of the panini grill.

[Other Good Indoor Grills]

Other good indoor grilling appliances include electric grills, such as those offered by Cuisinart and DeLonghi. Both these models are easy to use and provide high, direct heat similar to an outdoor grill. High heat is desirable because it sears the food, sealing in the juices. There is one potential drawback to high-heat cooking, however: the appliance may give off a large amount of smoke. I recommend using them under a vent hood to eliminate excessive smoke.

The grill plates on some of these models (the Cuisinart, specifically) reverse to a griddle side for a secondary style of cooking. In addition, the grills can accommodate a large amount of food, which eliminates the need for batch cooking.

[Grill Pans]

My favorite cooking appliance may be the cast iron grill pan. Although these pans are a bit more difficult to use than an electric appliance, cast iron pans offer superior searing and caramelization on the outside of the food. Outdoor grilling uses such high heat that foods sear almost instantly, trapping the juices and flavors inside. The closest thing to outdoor grilling indoors is a cast iron grill pan or a cast iron electric grill. This is because cast iron gets very hot and doesn't cool down when cold foods are placed on it. The main disadvantage to cast iron grill pans is the limited amount of cooking space. These pans generally measure 9" to 12" (23 to 30 cm) in diameter, giving you very little room to work with. You can counter this disadvantage, however, by grilling the food in batches and keeping cooked food warm in the oven.

Another alternative to a round cast iron pan is a long cast iron grilling/griddle pan. Like electric grilling appliances, these double-sided pans feature a grill on one side and a flat griddle on the other, offering two styles of cooking. There aren't really any disadvantages to these devices other than their weight: they can be quite cumbersome for someone with limited dexterity. Clean up is also very easy as long as the pan is well seasoned, as the seasoning essentially makes the pan nonstick.

If you're using a cast iron skillet, you should make sure the pan is properly seasoned. To season a cast iron pan, start by oiling it with vegetable or canola oil before preheating. After use, wipe or rinse it clean (don't use soap or a scouring pad) and dry it in a hot oven.

Last, oil it again lightly before storing. This repetitive oiling process gradually creates a nonstick coating on the pan; once you've achieved it, the pan is referred to as "seasoned." Preseasoned cast iron pans are a relatively recent invention and can be found in kitchen and houseware stores; be sure to follow the manufacturer's recommendations for care and storage prior to using these pans.

Simply put, some dishes are best made in a stovetop grill pan. While most electric grilling appliances are very versatile and easy to clean, certain dishes require the subtle nuances of stovetop cooking. Chicken fajitas, for example, can be made on an electric grill, but they are better when seared in a stovetop pan, where the high heat seals in the juices of the chicken and maintains the tenderness.

Storage space is another consideration when selecting an indoor grilling appliance. Many electric grilling appliances are cumbersome and take up a significant amount of countertop real estate. When purchasing, make sure you buy a model you have room for storing, whether that's on the countertop or wherever you store your other electric appliances.

[Stovetop Smokers and Wood Chips]

Developed as a way of preserving food before refrigeration, smoking foods today is a popular way of imparting robust, intense flavors on food while deepening their natural flavors. Although smoking has been used for centuries, it has made a comeback in restaurants and kitchens worldwide. Stovetop smokers are unique appliances, and are relatively new on the kitchen landscape. They allow you to bring what is typically an outdoor procedure indoors, making the technique of smoking available year round.

Not just a flavor-enhancing method, smoking foods is also a healthy way of cooking. With the modern cook inundated with pressure to cook lighter and healthier, it is encouraging to know that there is a method that can pack a tremendous flavor punch while still being good for you. Smoking foods allows you to prepare a meal using the natural juices and flavors of the food without adding any salt, fat, or oil during the cooking process.

Smoked foods are not standing in any fats during cooking—they are cooked on a rack within the smoking vessel—thus reducing the oils by 50 to 70 percent. While enhancing the inherent flavors of fish, poultry, meats, and vegetables, smoking also caramelizes foods, intensifying the flavor. Smoking can add unique essences to soy products, tofu, tempeh, or seitan ingredients, offering vegetarian eaters a simulated "meat" flavor. Asian cooking even utilizes tea leaves, herbs, and spices, combined with raw rice, for smoking everything from fowl to fish.

Throughout the testing and developing of these recipes I used the Cameron's Professional Stove-Top Smoker. Cameron's has a great variety of wood chips that they offer specifically for their smoker.

[Does the Wood Matter?]

Wood is as varied in its flavor offerings as herbs and spices are. While the variety of wood chips offered is ample, be sure to take into consideration which "flavor" of wood best complements the food being prepared. Created specifically for indoor, stovetop smokers, finely ground wood chips allow for quick smoking results, with intense flavor impact. Check with the maker of your stovetop smoker to ensure you are selecting the correct wood chips.

Listed here are the types of wood chips most readily available, with a brief description of their characteristics, and recommendations for their use.

Alder. Used most widely in the Pacific Northwest for smoking salmon, alder is a mild wood that adds a delicate smoky flavor to foods. Alder is best used with lighter foods, such as seafood and vegetables, as the flavor of the wood should not be too intense.

Apple. Fruitwoods have become quite popular for smoking, and apple is no exception. With a more complex flavor than alder, apple wood still offers a mild flavor best used on game, fish, and poultry.

Bourbon-soaked oak. To prepare this kind of wood, oak is soaked in real bourbon, absorbing its intense earthiness, then is dried and shredded for use in indoor smoking. The flavor is subtle, and is perfect for ribs, brisket, and other red meats.

Cherry. Another fruitwood that has become quite popular, cherry imparts a rich, smooth flavor, and pairs well with duck and other poultry.

Corncob. Consisting of the heart of the corncob, processed into small granules, this wood chip is not very common. Offering a lightly sweet, yet robust, flavor, corncob is best mixed with other complementary wood chips to intensify the flavors of chicken and pork.

Hickory. One of the most common wood chips, hickory is used for just about everything. A classic component of true barbecue, this hardwood adds depth with a smooth, even flavor that pairs perfectly with barbecue sauces.

Maple. A great wood for cheeses and vegetables, maple is a staple for subtle, dependable flavor.

Mesquite. Most popular in southwestern cooking, mesquite is another hardwood that packs a flavor punch. A little goes a long way here—if you overdo it, the food becomes bitter.

Oak. Widely used in commercial smoking, oak is a hardwood that is dependable and balanced in its flavors, and it pairs well with other wood varieties. A little goes a long way here, as well—use oak chips in moderation.

Pecan. Becoming more and more popular, pecan is a unique wood that creates a hearty robust smoke. Pecan pairs well with other woods as well; apple and pecan in particular give poultry, meats, and pork tremendous flavor.

corncob

alder

hickory

pecan

mesquite

cherry

bourbon-smoked oak

apple

chapter 2

Sauces, Glazes, Marinades, and Rubs

Many outdoor grilling and barbecue recipes include a marinade, rub, "mop," sauce, or glaze to add flavor, and indoor grilling is no different. Let's take a minute to discuss the differences among these flavor-enhancing mixtures.

[Marinade]

A marinade is a mix of herbs, spices, seasonings, oils, and citrus or vinegar that is designed to impart flavor and tenderize. Many marinades are used to tenderize especially tough cuts of meat, such as brisket or skirt steak. The citrus or vinegar in the marinade actually does the tenderizing, while the other ingredients pack flavor into the food. There isn't much need for tenderizing seafood and poultry, but citrus juices and vinegars can still be used to add great flavor to these foods.

[Dry Rubs]

Dry rubs combine sugars, spices, and herbs. Use them as marinades, but because they are dry instead of wet, you rub them all over the meat. This imparts flavor and creates a crust when cooked. A dry rub is a great way to get flavor to penetrate more deeply than a marinade, such as between the skin and flesh of poultry or massaged deep into the flesh of ribs or steaks. A dry rub is often topped with a "mop," or thick, chunky barbecue sauce, prior to cooking or during the grilling process. The flavors of dry rubs are literally endless; I have provided three rubs in this book, but it's easy to be creative and develop your own signature rub for grilling.

[Sauces, Glazes, and Mops]

Sauces and mops are designed for repeated use (such as basting) during the grilling or cooking process, adding flavor around the food. They are often used in slower outdoor grilling techniques such as barbecue. The sugars in sauces and mops often caramelize onto the food, creating a crust such as the one found on barbecued ribs. A mop is simply a heavier basting sauce with a catchy name derived from the moplike brush used to apply the sauce to the food. Glazes are also sauces, but they are applied after cooking and before serving.

Whatever the sauce, glaze, mop, rub, or marinade you select, they all add texture and flavor to grilled and smoked foods. Some sauces are best used with meat and poultry, while others are made specifically for seafood. Seafood, in general, needs a lighter marinade or sauce, while meat and poultry can withstand a heavier or even chunky sauce or marinade. One other note: this chapter isn't intended to imply that all grilled items need a sauce, rub, or marinade; sometimes grilled steak or shrimp is perfect just on its own.

[Brushes and Mops]

Utensils integral to basting during grilling, brushes and mops come in all sizes, shapes, and forms. (I have known cooks who simply use paint brushes from the hardware store.) When purchasing any brush or mop that will be used in food, pull on the bristles to ensure they are securely in place. Many less expensive brushes are of poor quality, and they leave bristles or brush hair on the food and in the sauce.

A unique, flavorful solution for brushing or mopping sauces is to use fresh herbs. Simply select hearty, sturdy herbs, such as sage, rosemary, or thyme, tie them together in a bunch with twine, and use them instead of a utensil. In addition to doubling as a brush or mop, this clever tool imparts its natural flavors on the foods during cooking. Herbs not suitable for this purpose are those that are tender and less sturdy, such as parsley, tarragon, dill, or chives.

Molasses BBQ Schmear

A "schmear," by my definition, is a thick and chunky barbecue sauce that doubles as a marinade or a basting sauce. This recipe combines the flavor of molasses with bacon and onion to make a sweet and smoky sauce that's perfect for ribs, beef, and poultry.

4 strips thick sliced bacon	3 tablespoons (32 g) dark brown sugar
1 large onion, finely chopped (about 2 cups [260 g])	1 tablespoon (15 ml) Worcestershire sauce
½ green bell pepper, finely chopped (about 1 cup [130 g])	1 tablespoon (15 g) prepared mustard
2 cloves (about 2 tablespoons [20 g]) garlic, minced	1 tablespoon (15 ml) cider vinegar
⅓ cup (100 g) molasses	½ teaspoon (3 ml) liquid smoke
¼ cup (63 g) prepared barbecue sauce	½ teaspoon (3 g) salt
¼ cup (60 g) ketchup	1 teaspoon (2 g) freshly ground black pepper

In a heavy pot, cook bacon over medium heat to render fat, about 5 minutes. Discard all but 3 tablespoons (45 ml) of the fat, reserving the bacon for another use. Add onion, pepper, and garlic and cook until vegetables are soft, about 5 minutes. Stir in molasses, barbecue sauce, ketchup, sugar, Worcestershire sauce, mustards, vinegar, and liquid smoke. Season with salt and black pepper. Simmer, uncovered, stirring occasionally, until thick, about 10 to 15 minutes. Remove from heat and let cool completely. Place in airtight jar or container and keep refrigerated for up to 2 weeks.

Rubs

Rubs are easy enhancements for grilled and smoked meats, poultry, game, and seafood. Simply a marriage of different herbs and spices, rubs provide a wide array of tremendous flavors.

[Makes about 1 cup (100 g)]

Spicy Dry Rub

¼ cup (28 g) sweet
Spanish paprika

2 tablespoons (18 g) ancho
chili powder

2 tablespoons (12 g)
coarse ground black pepper

2 tablespoons (18 g)
dry mustard

1 tablespoon (9 g)
garlic powder

½ tablespoon (9 g) salt

1 tablespoon (4 g) dried thyme

2 tablespoons (28 g)
brown sugar

1 teaspoon (2 g) ground cumin

1 teaspoon (2 g)
ground coriander

1 tablespoon (7 g) fennel seeds

Combine all ingredients in small mixing bowl, working with fork or fingers to mix well. Place in airtight container or jar and store for up to 1 month.

[Makes about 1½ cups (150 g)]

Sweet Chili Rub

½ cup (100 g) sugar

¼ cup (56 g) light brown sugar

1 tablespoon (9 g) dry mustard

2 tablespoons (18 g) chili powder

1 tablespoon (9 g) chipotle
chili powder (substitute ancho
chili powder for a milder taste)

1 tablespoon (18 g) salt

2 tablespoon (12 g) coarse
ground black pepper

Combine all ingredients in small mixing bowl, working with fork or fingers to mix well. Place in airtight container or jar and store for up to 1 month.

[Makes about ⅔ cup (67 g)]

Cajun Dry Rub

2 tablespoons (14 g) paprika

2 tablespoons (36 g) salt

2 tablespoons (18 g) garlic powder

1 teaspoon (2 g) white pepper

1 tablespoon (9 g) ground
dried bay leaves or filé powder

1 tablespoon (9 g) onion powder

1 tablespoon (6 g) cayenne pepper

2 tablespoons (8 g) dried oregano

1 tablespoon (4 g) dried thyme

1 tablespoon (13 g) sugar

Combine all ingredients in small mixing bowl, working with fork or fingers to mix well. Place in airtight container or jar and store for up to 1 month.

[Makes about 2 cups (475 ml)]

Sweet Mustard Grilling "Mop" (Sauce)

A "mop" is a barbecue basic that adds layers of flavor to barbecue recipes throughout the slow cooking process. For indoor grilling purposes, this mop adds layers of flavor working as a marinade.

2 tablespoons (28 g) butter

½ cup (125 g) yellow sweet onion, chopped

3 cloves (about 3 tablespoons [30 g]) fresh garlic, minced

1 teaspoon (2 g) paprika

¼ teaspoon (5 mg) ground nutmeg

1 teaspoon (2 g) chili powder

⅓ cup (80 g) yellow prepared mustard

1 tablespoon (9 g) Coleman's mustard

1 cup (235 ml) bottled Italian salad dressing

1 tablespoon (15 ml) Worcestershire sauce

1 tablespoon (15 ml) lime juice

1 tablespoon (20 g) honey

1 teaspoon (4 g) sugar

Salt and black pepper to taste

In a medium saucepan, melt butter over medium heat. Add onion and garlic and sauté until onion is tender and transparent (but not brown), about 7 minutes. Remove from heat and transfer to the bowl of a food processor fitted with the blade attachment, then pulse to purée mixture into a paste. Return mixture to saucepan over medium heat, add paprika, nutmeg, and chili powder, stirring to combine, and toast spices until aromatic, about 3 minutes. Add mustards, Italian dressing, Worcestershire sauce, lime juice, honey, and sugar, and bring mixture to a boil. Season with salt and pepper to taste, then remove from heat and cool. This sauce can be covered and refrigerated for up to 2 weeks.

Dark Ale Grilling Sauce

Beer is a great tenderizer and adds nice flavor to meat and poultry. This "mop," or barbecue sauce, works well as a marinade or a basting sauce for grilling meat and poultry.

1 (12-ounce [355 ml]) bottle dark ale

1/2 cup (120 ml) cider vinegar

1/4 cup (60 ml) vegetable oil

2 tablespoons (30 ml) Worcestershire sauce

2 tablespoons (30 g) minced jalapeño chilies

1 cup (250 g) prepared barbecue sauce

1 tablespoon (18 g) chili powder

1 teaspoon (3 g) ancho chili powder

1 teaspoon (3 g) paprika

1/4 cup (50 g) dark brown sugar

1/2 teaspoon (3 g) salt

1 teaspoon (6 g) coarse ground black pepper

1 tablespoon (8 g) corn starch

2 tablespoons (30 ml) water

Combine all but the last two ingredients in saucepan over medium-high heat. Bring to boil, reduce heat to simmer, and cook for 10 minutes. Dissolve cornstarch in water in a small bowl. Add cornstarch mixture to boiling sauce and stir to thicken. Cook sauce for an additional 5 minutes. Remove from heat and let cool. The sauce can be stored in an airtight container or jar and kept refrigerated for up to 2 weeks.

Roasted **Garlic and Cumin Sauce**

Roasted garlic has quite a different flavor than fresh garlic: it is very intense and concentrated. This recipe roasts the garlic with balsamic vinegar and cumin, packing even more flavor into the little cloves.

2 heads whole garlic, ½" (0.6 cm) cut away from top

¼ cup (60 ml) balsamic vinegar

1 teaspoon (6 g) ground cumin

1 (14-ounce [425 ml]) can tomato sauce

2 tablespoons (28 g) brown sugar

1 tablespoon (20 g) tomato paste

1 tablespoon (9 g) dry mustard

1 tablespoon (15 g) prepared Dijon mustard

2 tablespoons (30 ml) Worcestershire sauce

1 teaspoon (2 g) coarse ground black pepper

Preheat oven to 350°F (180°C). Coat a shallow 9" (23 cm) square baking dish with nonstick cooking spray. Place garlic heads in dish with cut side facing up. Slowly drizzle garlic with balsamic vinegar so it seeps between cloves, then top with cumin. Cover with aluminum foil and roast on middle rack of oven until brown and tender, about 45 minutes. Remove from oven and let cool. When the garlic is cool enough to handle, squeeze roasted garlic out of each clove by pressing from bottom of clove between two fingers. Squeeze roasted garlic into a bowl and add balsamic vinegar from roasting pan. In a small saucepan over medium heat, combine tomato sauce, brown sugar, tomato paste, dry and Dijon mustards, Worcestershire sauce, black pepper, and roasted garlic paste. Bring to a boil, then reduce heat and cook for 15 minutes. Remove from heat and let cool completely. Place in airtight container or jar and keep refrigerated for up to 2 weeks.

[Makes about ½ cup (120 g)]

Roasted **Garlic**

Roasting garlic concentrates the flavors of raw garlic into an intense, robust, earthy flavor and aroma. Like truffle oil, the flavor and smell of roasted garlic is distinctive and easily recognizable. If you don't like the taste of raw garlic, I encourage you to try this technique, as roasted garlic is unique and enjoyable.

4 heads fresh garlic, stem ends removed to ½" (1.25 cm)

2 tablespoons (30 ml) olive oil

Salt

Coarse ground black pepper

Preheat the oven to 375°F (190°C). Place the garlic, cut ends facing up, in an oven-safe pan or dish. Drizzle each head with olive oil and season with salt and pepper. Cover, then place in oven and roast for 30 to 45 minutes or until garlic is a rich brown, caramelized color and the cloves are easily pierced with the sharp tip of a knife. Remove from oven and let cool. If not using immediately, store refrigerated in an airtight container for up to 1 week. If using immediately, remove the roasted cloves by pinching the ends of each clove to force the garlic from the skin.

chapter 3

Grilled **Beginnings:**
Appetizers, Soups,
and Salads

One of the greatest joys of indoor grilling and smoking is the ease by which everything can be prepared, cooked, and served. This chapter is all about those great dishes that either start a meal or serve as the highlights of a cocktail party. By design, most of the recipes in this chapter are simple to execute and can be prepared ahead of time. In addition, they need only a quick finishing touch before your guests arrive.

This chapter is also about using your grill pan, appliance, and or indoor smoker to create unique and special dishes. Recipes such as Smoked Brie with Roasted Garlic and Browned Butter (page 35), Smoked Shrimp Martini with Mango Salad (page 38), or Grilled Potato Salad (page 45) are classic ideas with a twist. Serve the smoked shrimp cocktail in an elegant martini glass to give an old standby a modern look. As with all my recipes, use them as is, or as ideas to spark your own creativity in the kitchen. I encourage you to use these recipes as a springboard for your own recipes and creations.

Griddle Cakes with Cherry-Smoked Salmon and Red Onions

This dish requires several steps and a bit of preparation, but the finished product is quite delicious. If you are using this recipe as a party appetizer, prepare everything in advance and compose the actual dish just before your guests arrive.

FOR THE GRIDDLE CAKES:

1 cup (138 g) Johnny cake white cornmeal

1 tsp (5g) sugar

½ tsp (3 g) salt

½ cups (355 ml) water, boiling

Vegetable oil for cooking

FOR THE CHERRY-SMOKED SALMON:

1 salmon fillet (about ½ pound [225 g]) with skin intact

1 tablespoon (6 g) coarse ground black pepper

1 tablespoon (19 g) kosher salt

¼ teaspoon (0.5 g) ground nutmeg

1 teaspoon (2 g) cumin seeds

1 teaspoon (2 g) fennel seeds

2 tablespoons (28 g) light brown sugar

1 tablespoon (9 g) dry mustard

2 tablespoons (28 g) cherry wood chips for stovetop smoker

FOR THE TART RED ONIONS:

1 large red onion, cut in half, peeled, and thinly sliced

1 tablespoon (14 g) butter

1 tablespoon (15 ml) olive oil

½ cup (120 ml) red wine vinegar

¼ cup (60 ml) white balsamic vinegar

Salt and black pepper to taste

1 tablespoon (4 g) chopped fresh parsley

1 teaspoon (1 g) chopped fresh tarragon

2 tablespoons (30 g) sour cream

Combine cornmeal with sugar and salt in large mixing bowl. Add boiling water, and mix well. The batter will be thick.

For the salmon, combine black pepper, nutmeg, salt, anise, brown sugar, and mustard in small mixing bowl. Place salmon on large platter and rub thoroughly with dry spice mixture, coating evenly and completely. Place wood chips in bottom of a stovetop smoker, cover with smoking rack, spray rack and drip tray with nonstick cooking spray, and close lid. Place smoker on burner over medium heat until smoke begins to form, about 5 minutes. Working quickly, remove lid of smoker, place salmon on smoking rack, skin side down, and close lid. Smoke salmon for 20 minutes. Remove from heat and set aside, without opening smoker, for 15 additional minutes.

Meanwhile, heat stovetop cast iron griddle (or electric griddle) to medium-high heat (about 375°F [190°C]). Add 2 tablespoons (30 ml) vegetable oil to griddle. Working in batches, spoon a large spoonful of Johnny cake batter onto griddle and press with bottom of spoon to flatten into a disc about 1½" (4 cm) wide and ¼" (5 mm) thick. Cook until browned on both sides, about 3 minutes per side. Remove and set aside.

For the tart red onions, melt the butter with the oil in a large saucepan over high heat, then add onions and sauté until just tender, but not brown. Add vinegars, brown sugar, salt, and pepper and continue cooking until liquid is reduced by half. Remove from heat, add parsley and tarragon, and stir to combine. To assemble griddle cakes, top with a small chunk of smoked salmon, a dollop of sour cream, and a scoop of tart red onions. Serve warm.

A Johnny Cake by Any Other Name...

Referred to regionally as ashcakes, battercakes, corn cakes, hoecakes, journey cakes, or Shawnee cakes, Johnny cakes have been a quintessential New England treat since the mid 1800s. No matter the name, they are simply a combination of boiled water, salt, and cornmeal, mixed just until moistened, and griddle fried (preferably on cast iron). (They can also be baked into little "cakes" in the oven.) White cornmeal—specifically, Kenyon's Stone Ground White, if you can find it—is ideal, though yellow cornmeal will do. The recipe given here suggests the miniature cakes be cooked for 3 minutes per side. For larger cakes, cook batter on griddle for 6 minutes, undisturbed. Turn cake over, and cook for an additional 8 to 10 minutes until golden.

To experiment with Johnny cakes, add herbs or other ingredients and flavors to the batter itself; or serve the cakes with a variety of toppings and accompaniments to complement any meal—or any course. These treats have stood the test of both time and culinary trends, and are an excellent addition to any cook's repertoire.

To learn where to buy Kenyon's Stone Ground White Cornmeal, you can contact the Usquepough, Rhode Island, Company at (401) 783-4054.

Smoked **Brie with Roasted Garlic and Browned Butter**

Brie is a soft, mild, spreadable cheese that is quite popular as an appetizer. I enjoy Brie in many presentations, whether spread on a crositini or layered in a sandwich. This method of smoking Brie infuses robust, intense flavors into the cheese. You can serve this Brie as an appetizer at a cocktail party or use it to flavor other foods or recipes, such as cut into small wedges and served over green salad.

1 (1 pound [455 g]) Brie wheel (not a wedge)

2 tablespoons (28 g) cherry wood chips for stovetop smoker

1/4 cup (55 g) butter

1 head roasted garlic (see technique page 28)

1/4 cup (32 g) slivered almonds

1 soft French baguette, sliced in 1/4" (5 mm)-thick diagonal slices

Remove Brie from packaging and carefully cut away the top layer of the cheese's velvety white coating using a serrated knife. (Brie must be refrigerated ahead of time to remove the top layer most easily.) Place cherry wood chips in bottom of stovetop smoker, cover with smoking rack, spray rack and drip tray with nonstick cooking spray, and close lid. Place smoker on burner over medium heat until smoke begins to form, about 5 minutes. Place Brie, cut side up, on cooking rack, close smoker, and smoke for 20 minutes. Remove Brie from smoker and set aside until the Brie becomes firm. Note: the Brie should not get hot enough to melt and ooze. If the smoker appears too hot (you will notice a heavy sizzling sound), reduce the heat.

Meanwhile, melt butter over medium-high heat in a medium skillet, then add roasted garlic cloves and slivered almonds. Cook until butter begins to brown and almonds begin toasting, about 5 minutes. Place Brie on a serving plate, then pour browned butter over top of Brie. Serve warm with sliced bread.

The Brie can be reheated, uncovered, in a low-temperature oven if necessary. If using Brie in other presentations, omit preparation of browned butter and roasted garlic, allow Brie to cool after smoking, wrap tightly, and refrigerate until ready to use.

1 pound (455 g) chorizo sausage links

1 tablespoon (14 g) mesquite wood chips for stovetop smoker

4 slices smoked bacon, chopped

1 medium red onion, chopped fine

1 red pepper, chopped

1 green pepper, chopped

2 tablespoons (20 g) minced fresh garlic

1 Serrano chili, seeded and chopped fine

1 Anaheim chili, seeded and chopped fine

1 (12-ounce [355 ml]) bottle dark beer

$\frac{1}{8}$ teaspoon (4 mg) ground cinnamon

3 tablespoons (27g) ground cumin

2 teaspoons (6 g) ground coriander

2 tablespoons (18 g) chili powder

2 (15.5-ounce [430 ml]) cans black beans; 1 can partially drained and 1 can undrained

1 (14.5-ounce [406 ml]) can beef stock

3 tablespoons (12 g) fresh chopped cilantro, 1 tablespoon (4 g) reserved for garnish

1 teaspoon (5 ml) hot sauce

1 tablespoon (15 ml) fresh lime juice

$1\frac{1}{2}$ teaspoons (3 g) fresh ground black pepper

1 teaspoon (6 g) salt

8 ounces (113 g) shredded cheddar cheese

$\frac{1}{2}$ cup (115 g) sour cream

Corn tortilla chips

[Serves 6 as a starter or 4 as a meal]

Black Bean Chili with Grilled Chorizo

I love any kind of chili, especially a meaty, hearty version with beans and fresh vegetables. Topped with melted cheese and served with buttery crackers, there's no better definition of comfort food. Enjoy this chili as a hearty dinner or as a precursor to a lighter grilled dinner.

Place wood chips in bottom of stovetop smoker, cover with smoking rack, spray rack and drip tray with nonstick cooking spray, and close lid. Place smoker on burner over medium heat until smoke begins to form, about 5 minutes.

Place chorizo links on rack, close lid, and smoke links for 20 minutes. Remove smoker from heat, then uncover and transfer chorizo to cutting board. When cool enough to handle, cut chorizo into large chunks.

In large stockpot, cook bacon over high heat, until crisp and fat is rendered, about 7 minutes. Remove bacon and set aside on paper towel to drain. Add onion, peppers, garlic, and chili peppers to bacon grease and sauté until vegetables are tender, about 5 minutes. Add the chorizo, cooking and stirring for 3 minutes. Add beer and stir to heat through until foam subsides.

Add the cumin, coriander, chili powder, and cinnamon, and cook and stir for an additional 5 minutes.

Meanwhile, empty the partially drained can of black beans into mixing bowl. Using hands or a fork, crush beans into a paste. Add the undrained can of beans and bean paste to stock pot and stir to combine. Using a potato masher or the back of a large spoon, crush some beans in the pot to add thickness. Stir to combine, scraping bottom of pot. Reduce heat to simmer, add the hot sauce, lime juice, beef broth, and 2 tablespoons (8 g) of the cilantro, stir, and cook for 10 minutes, stirring occasionally. Add beef broth and cilantro and stir. Cook for 20 additional minutes. To serve, garnish with cheddar cheese, a dollop of sour cream, sprinkle of cilantro, reserved crumbled bacon, and crumbled corn chips.

Smoked **Shrimp Martini** with **Mango Salad**

There are very few things as indulgent as a chilled shrimp cocktail. This modern redo pairs smoked shrimp, red onion, and mango salad in a martini glass.

16 jumbo shrimp (size 13/15), about 1 pound (455 g), peeled and deveined

1 tablespoon (14 g) alder wood chips

1 avocado, peeled and diced

1 mango, peeled and diced

1/4 cup (15 g) packed basil leaves, torn into small pieces

2 tablespoons (28 ml) fresh lime juice

1 jalapeño pepper, seeded and minced

Salt and black pepper to taste

1 cup (20 g) mixed micro greens or mesclun mix

1 cup (240 g) Horseradish Cocktail Sauce (recipe follows)

FOR HORSERADISH COCKTAIL SAUCE:

Makes about 1 1/3 cups (320 g)

1 cup (240 g) ketchup

2 tablespoons (28 ml) mango nectar

2 tablespoons (30 g) ground horseradish

2 tablespoons (30 ml) fresh lemon juice

2 teaspoons (4 g) lemon zest

1 dash hot sauce

Set up stovetop smoker with alder wood chips in bottom, then return drip tray to smoker and add 1 cup (235 ml) water. Top with food rack. Rinse shrimp and position on food rack. Close smoker lid, place on burner over medium heat, and smoke shrimp for 20 minutes. When smoking is complete, remove shrimp and plunge into ice-cold water. Remove from water, peel, devein, and chill in refrigerator until ready to serve, at least 1 hour.

Meanwhile, combine avocado, mango, basil, lime juice, and jalapeño pepper in small bowl, season with salt and pepper, stir to combine, then cover and refrigerate for at least 30 minutes. Serve shrimp in a martini glass filled with greens, avocado salad, and Horseradish Cocktail Sauce; garnish with lime wedge.

[For Horseradish Cocktail Sauce]
Combine all ingredients in small bowl and stir to combine. Cover and refrigerate until ready to serve, at least 1 hour. The sauce can be made in advance and refrigerated in airtight container or jar for up to 1 week.

Alder-Smoked **Lemon-Pepper Bluefish**

Bluefish is a moderately oily fish with great texture that is perfect for smoking. High in omega-3 fatty acids, bluefish is also a healthy choice. This recipe is as good as it is simple. Simply oil the fish and coat it with lemon pepper and the wood chips will do the rest of the work.

1 pound (455 g) bluefish fillets, skin left intact

2 tablespoons (28 ml) olive oil

⅓ cup (32 g) lemon pepper seasoning

2 tablespoons (28 g) alder wood chips

Place bluefish fillets on large sheet pan and brush each fillet evenly with olive oil, then sprinkle each thoroughly with lemon pepper. Place wood chips in bottom of stovetop smoker, cover with smoking rack, and spray rack and drip tray with nonstick cooking spray. Position bluefish fillets, skin side down, on rack, close lid, and place smoker on burner over medium heat. Smoke bluefish for 30 minutes, then remove from heat and, without opening lid, let stand for 10 minutes. Remove lid and transfer bluefish fillets to platter to cool. Serve or use in recipe variations that follow.

Variations

[Smoked Bluefish Spread]
Flake 1 smoked bluefish fillet, then combine with 16 ounces (460 g) sour cream, ½ cup (112 g) mayonnaise, ¼ cup (25 g) finely chopped scallions, and 3 tablespoons (45 ml) lemon juice in bowl. Mix using fork. Serve with whole wheat or stone wheat crackers.

[Smoked Bluefish and Pasta]
Boil your favorite pasta until al dente. Sauté 3 cloves minced garlic with 2 chopped shallots and ½ cup (56 g) chopped pecans in 3 tablespoons (45 ml) olive oil and 2 tablespoons (28 g) butter until garlic and onion are tender and pecans are aromatic. Add 1 cup (235 ml) dry white wine, 1 flaked smoked bluefish fillet, 2 teaspoons (4 g) lemon zest, and 1 tablespoon (15 ml) lemon juice. Reduce mixture for 3 minutes, then toss with cooked pasta and garnish with freshly grated Parmesan cheese and fresh chopped Italian parsley. Serve warm.

Smoked **Tomato and Grilled Onion Crostini with Lemon Bagna Cauda**

This northern Italian sauce originated as a "hot bath" for raw vegetables but is also excellent over grilled fish or served as a condiment. Zuni Café, in San Francisco, makes a delicious version of this recipe as an appetizer. My adaptation uses smoked tomatoes on crostini, almost like a bruschetta.

FOR THE CROSTINI:

4 large plum tomatoes, cut in half lengthwise

3 tablespoons (45 ml) extra-virgin olive oil, plus extra for brushing

1 tablespoon (14 g) maple wood chips

1 small, sweet yellow onion, sliced thick

Freshly ground black pepper to taste

1 tablespoon (15 ml) balsamic vinegar

1 tablespoon (4 g) chopped fresh tarragon

1 tablespoon (4 g) chopped fresh basil

1 large Parisian loaf or French baguette, sliced into ¼" (5 mm)-thick diagonal slices

1 recipe Lemon Bagna Cauda (recipe follows)

FOR THE LEMON BAGNA CAUDA:

Makes about 1 cup (235 ml)

¹/₄ small lemon, plus additional lemon juice to taste

2 cloves garlic, chopped

³/₄ cup (175 ml) extra-virgin olive oil

3 tablespoons (43 g) chopped salt-packed anchovy fillets (about 14 fillets)

2 tablespoons (18 g) pine nuts

Fresh cracked black pepper

Place maple wood chips on bottom of stovetop smoker and return drip pan and smoking rack to smoker. Spray smoking rack with nonstick cooking spray. Place tomatoes, cut side face up, on smoking rack, sprinkle each with olive oil (use only 1 tablespoon (15 ml) oil in all), and season with black pepper. Close smoker lid and place on burner over medium heat. Smoke tomatoes for 10 to 12 minutes.

Meanwhile, preheat stovetop grill pan or electric grill to high heat. Brush sliced onion with 1 tablespoon (15 ml) olive oil and season with black pepper. Place onion on grilling surface and cook until brown and tender, about 5 minutes per side. Remove and set aside to cool. Remove tomatoes from smoker and set aside to cool. When cool enough to handle, chop tomatoes and onions and place in mixing bowl. Add remaining balsamic vinegar, remaining olive oil, tarragon, and basil and stir to combine. Season with salt and pepper, then cover and refrigerate for at least 30 minutes.

Meanwhile, preheat stovetop grill pan or electric grill to high heat. Brush both sides of sliced bread generously with olive oil and grill until brown and toasted, about 6 minutes on each side. Serve grilled bread topped with smoked tomato and onion mixture and 1 teaspoon (5 ml) Lemon Bagna Cauda.

[For the Lemon Bagna Cauda]
Cut lemons into thin slices and remove seeds. Chop lemon into coarse chunks. In a small saucepan, combine lemon with garlic and about half of the olive oil. Cook over low heat until oil is hot, then remove from heat and let cool. Add anchovies and remaining oil, stir, and reheat until warm. Set aside.

Preheat oven to 300°F (150°C). Spread pine nuts in single layer on baking sheet, place in oven, and toast, about 6 minutes. Pound or chop pine nuts into a crumbly paste, add to warm lemon sauce, and stir to combine. Season with black pepper and add additional lemon juice if needed to thin. Adjust seasonings and stir just before serving.

Grilled **Shrimp Salad with Citrus, Almonds, and Watermelon**

Watermelon is a summertime favorite that inspires many thoughts of outdoor grilling. If we can bring the grill indoors, then we can bring watermelon to a salad. Watermelon is an excellent accompaniment to grilled shrimp.

Combine soy sauce, honey, Worcestershire sauce, orange juice, orange zest, olive oil, salt, and black pepper in large mixing bowl and whisk together. Add shrimp and toss to coat thoroughly, then cover and refrigerate for at least 1 hour.

Meanwhile, toast almonds in a 375°F (190°C) oven until just brown and aromatic, about 10 minutes. Remove and set aside. Melt butter with olive oil in small skillet over medium heat. Add toasted almonds, lemon juice, Worcestershire sauce, and brown sugar, then toss to coat almonds and cook until bubbling, about 5 minutes. Remove from heat and set aside.

1½ pounds (680 g) jumbo shrimp (size 13/15), peeled and deveined

½ cup (120 ml) soy sauce

3 tablespoons (60 g) honey

2 teaspoons (10 ml) Worcestershire sauce

Juice of one orange (about ¼ cup [60 ml])

Zest of one orange

¼ cup (60 ml) extra-virgin olive oil

½ teaspoon (3 g) salt

1 teaspoon (6 g) coarse ground black pepper

¼ (32 g) cup sliced almonds, toasted

1 tablespoon (14 g) butter

1 tablespoon (15 ml) olive oil

1 tablespoon (15 ml) lemon juice

1 teaspoon (5 ml) Worcestershire sauce

1 tablespoon (14 g) brown sugar

12 ounces (340 g) mixed salad greens

2 cups (400 g) chopped watermelon

6 ounces (168 g) crumbled goat cheese

FOR THE CHAMPAGNE VINAIGRETTE:

Makes about 1 cup (235 ml)

¼ cup (60 ml) champagne vinegar

¼ cup (60 ml) fresh squeezed orange juice

1 tablespoon (20 g) honey

1 teaspoon (4 g) sugar

½ teaspoon (3 g) salt

½ teaspoon (1 g) black pepper

½ cup (120 ml) extra-virgin olive oil

2 tablespoons (8 g) fresh chopped Italian flat-leaf parsley

1 tablespoon (4 g) fresh chopped tarragon

[For the Vinaigrette]
Combine all ingredients except parsley and tarragon in the bowl of a food processor fitted with the blade attachment. Process until well combined and thick, then add parsley and tarragon and adjust seasonings as needed and set aside.

Remove shrimp from refrigerator and bring to room temperature. Preheat stovetop grill pan or electric grill to high heat. Spray pan or grill with nonstick cooking spray, place shrimp on grill pan and cook until brown and cooked through, turning once, about 5 minutes per side. Remove and set aside to cool.

Toss greens and watermelon with ¼ cup (60 ml) of salad dressing in large salad bowl. In a separate bowl or dish toss shrimp with ¼ cup (60 ml) of salad dressing. Place individual servings of greens and watermelon on plates, top with grilled shrimp, then sprinkle with almonds and goat cheese. Serve remaining salad dressing on the side.

Grilled **Potato Salad**

Potato salad is a summertime favorite—with as many variations as there are summer days. This version, with grilled potatoes, can be enjoyed all year long, rain or shine.

2 pounds (910 g) (about 6 medium sized) red potatoes, sliced into 1" (2.5 cm)-thick rounds

3 tablespoons (45 ml) olive oil

1 tablespoon (15 ml) balsamic vinegar

1 tablespoon (7 g) paprika

1 teaspoon (1 g) oregano

½ teaspoon (3 g) salt

1 teaspoon (2 g) black pepper

2 cups (475 ml) ranch dressing

6 slices bacon, fried and chopped

1 large red onion, chopped

4 scallions, thinly sliced, green and white parts

3 cloves (about 3 tablespoons [30 g]) fresh garlic, minced

Place potatoes in large pot and add just enough water to fully cover potatoes by 4" (10 cm). Bring potatoes to boil. Continue to boil until potatoes are tender but still firm, about 15 minutes.

Meanwhile, combine olive oil, balsamic vinegar, paprika, oregano, salt, and pepper in the bowl of a blender or food processor, then pulse to combine. Remove potatoes from heat, drain, and set aside to cool. When cool enough to handle, place potato in mixing bowl, toss with olive oil mixture, and set aside. Preheat stovetop grill pan or electric grill to medium-high heat. Grill potatoes until brown and tender, about 7 minutes on each side if using grill pan, or 7 minutes total on electric grill with lid. Return potatoes to original mixing bowl and toss with half of the ranch dressing. Add remaining ingredients and remaining ranch dressing, toss to combine, cover, and refrigerate for at least 1 hour.

[Serves 6]

Grilled **Scallop Salad with Oranges and Strawberries**

Strawberries are not just for sweet concoctions. Their mildly tart flavor and sweet ripeness lend them to many uses. Here, I have combined strawberries with sweet grilled scallops and fennel, which are all enhanced by the citrus burst of navel oranges.

10 ounces (250 g) mixed salad greens (arugula, mesclun mix, watercress, or other greens of your choice)

1 cup (110 g) strawberries, stemmed and quartered

2 navel oranges, peeled, cut in half vertically, and sliced into ¼" (5 mm)-thick slices

⅓ cup (45 g) toasted pine nuts (optional, see page 43 for recipe)

1 pound (455 g) large bay scallops

2 heads fennel (tops removed), cut into ¼" (5 mm)-thick wedges

2 tablespoons (30 ml) olive oil

Salt and black pepper to taste

1 cup (235 ml) Citrus Tarragon Vinaigrette (recipe follows)

FOR VINAIGRETTE:

Makes about 1½ cups (355 ml)

1 cup (235 ml) freshly squeezed orange juice

3 tablespoons (45 ml) cider vinegar

1 tablespoon (15 g) Dijon mustard

¼ cup (60 ml) extra-virgin olive oil

2 tablespoons (30 g) sugar

2 tablespoons (30 g) fresh tarragon, chopped

[For the Vinaigrette]
In the bowl of a food processor fitted with the blade attachment, combine orange juice with cider vinegar and Dijon mustard; pulse to mix the ingredients. With the processor running, add the olive oil in a steady stream, to emulsify the dressing. Remove from processor, add sugar and tarragon, and stir to combine and dissolve the sugar. Refrigerate until needed.

[To Assemble Salad]
In a large bowl, combine mixed greens with strawberries and oranges. Cover and refrigerate until ready to use. If using toasted pine nuts, toast according to directions (see page 43), and set aside until needed.

Make Tarragon Citrus Vinaigrette dressing (recipe at right) and refrigerate until needed.

In a small bowl, toss the scallops with 2 tablespoons (30 ml) of the vinaigrette; cover and refrigerate for at least 30 minutes. Preheat a stovetop, electric, or other indoor grill pan set over high heat. Toss the fennel with the olive oil, and season with salt and black pepper. Place fennel in the grill pan, and cook until browned and tender, about 8 minutes per side. Remove fennel and set aside to cool. Retrieve scallops from the refrigerator and grill until browned, about 3 or 4 minutes per side. Remove from grill and set aside to cool. In a large bowl, toss the salad greens with the remaining vinaigrette, plate individual portions of the greens, and top each serving with scallops and fennel. Sprinkle with toasted pine nuts, if desired, and serve.

Grilled **Chicken Wings with Hot and Sweet Dipping Sauces**

Who doesn't enjoy eating sticky but tender chicken wings with dipping sauce? Plan on getting your fingers messy with these stovetop grilled wings. Game day will never be the same!

12 whole chicken wings

1/3 cup (33 g) Cajun Dry Rub or Spicy Dry Rub (see recipes, page 24)

2 large carrots, peeled and cut into sticks

2 large stalks celery, cut into sticks

1/2 cup (125 ml) Molasses BBQ Schmear (recipe page 23)

1/2 cup (125 ml) Sweet Mustard Grilling "Mop" (recipe page 25)

Wash chicken wings thoroughly, then drain and pat them dry. Toss chicken wings with either of the dry rubs in a large mixing bowl, coating evenly. For hotter wings, coat even heavier with dry rub. Cover and refrigerate for 24 hours. Remove from refrigerator, then preheat stovetop grill or electric grill to high heat. Spray pan or grill with nonstick cooking spray. Place wings on grill and cook until brown and crisp on all sides, about 15 minutes, turning a few times. Remove and serve with dipping sauce and carrot and celery sticks.

To vary the flavor for this chicken wing recipe, combine 2 or more other dry rubs in this book. For a cool dipping sauce, serve with prepared honey Dijon dressing or blue cheese dressing.

Grilled **Vegetable Egg Rolls**

This recipe for vegetable egg rolls makes a nice vegetarian meal. Grilling vegetables adds great, intense flavor and really highlights their freshness.

2 zucchini, washed

2 yellow summer squash, washed

2 large carrots, peeled

6 asparagus spears

Olive oil

2 cups (70 g) shredded Napa cabbage

1 cup (75 g) snow peas, thinly shredded

6 sheets egg roll wraps

1 egg beaten with 1 tablespoon (15 ml) water

Vegetable oil for frying

Ginger-Balsamic Dipping Sauce (recipe follows)

½ cup (120 g) prepared duck sauce

FOR GINGER-BALSAMIC DIPPING SAUCE:

Makes about 1 cup (235 ml)

½ cup (120 ml) soy sauce

¼ cup (60 ml) balsamic vinegar

1 tablespoon (16 g) Chinese fish sauce

3 tablespoons (60 g) honey

2 tablespoons (16 g) freshly grated ginger

1 clove garlic, minced (about 1 tablespoon [10 g])

½ teaspoon (3 g) salt

½ teaspoon (1 g) black pepper

Slice zucchini and yellow squash into ¼" (5 mm)-thick slices lengthwise. Using vegetable peeler, gently peel away outer skin of asparagus spears, then break off and discard tough ends. Brush vegetables generously with olive oil. Preheat a stovetop grill pan or electric grill to high heat. Grill vegetables until tender and browned, about 10 minutes, turning during grilling. Remove and set aside to cool. Once cool enough to handle, slice vegetables into thin strips and set aside.

Pour vegetable oil in large saucepan or stockpot, 4" (10 cm) deep. Heat oil to 375°F (190°C). Working on a flat surface, place egg roll wraps in front of you with one point facing you. Working in equal batches, place assorted sliced grilled vegetables, cabbage, and snow peas in the center of the wrap. Brush edges with egg wash. Fold in sides and roll egg rolls away from you, ensuring sides are sticking and sealing vegetables in. Apply additional egg wash, if needed. Repeat process until egg rolls are complete. Working in batches, if necessary, place egg rolls gently into hot oil. Fry them until they are golden brown, about 4 minutes. Remove and set on paper towel to drain. Serve warm with Ginger-Balsamic Dipping Sauce and duck sauce.

[For Ginger-Balsamic Dipping Sauce]
Combine all ingredients in bowl using whisk. Cover and refrigerate until ready to use.

chapter 4

Meat

4 rib-eye steaks, 1" to 1 1/2" (2.5 to 4 cm) thick

1 tablespoon (14 g) unsalted butter

1/2 cup (80 g) minced ciopolin onions or shallots

2 cloves (about 2 tablespoons [20 g]) garlic, minced

1/3 cup (42 ml) brandy

2 cups (475 ml) beef broth

1 tablespoon (5 g) black peppercorns, crushed

1 tablespoon (5 g) green peppercorns, crushed

1/3 cup (42 ml) heavy cream

4 teaspoons (11 g) cornstarch

1 tablespoon (15 g) whole-grain mustard

2 teaspoons (2 g) chopped fresh tarragon

[For the Steaks]

Preheat stovetop grill pan over burner on medium-high heat. Grill steaks to desired doneness (medium-rare is suggested), about 6 minutes per side. Remove steaks from pan, place on plate, and set aside. Save pan drippings for sauce.

[For the Sauce]

In separate skillet, heat pan drippings from grilled steaks with 1 tablespoon (14 ml) butter, add onion and minced garlic, and cook for 1 to 2 minutes. Deglaze pan with brandy, scraping up any brown bits that stick to skillet. Add beef broth and peppercorns to pan. Combine heavy cream and cornstarch in small bowl, then whisk cornstarch mixture into sauce and simmer until thickened, about 5 minutes. Add mustard and any remaining juices from steak plate and stir to combine. Serve steaks warm with peppercorn sauce.

[Makes 4 servings]

Pan-Grilled **Rib-Eye Steaks with Brandy Peppercorn Sauce**

A simple grilled steak has no competition as a great meal. Add a flavorful velvety sauce and you've got a real winner. This recipe tops tender grilled rib-eye steaks with a spicy peppercorn and brandy sauce. For the best results when grilling steak, be sure to buy the highest quality meat you can afford from a reputable butcher.

Grilled **New Zealand Lamb Chops with Cilantro-Mint Glaze**

Lamb chops grilled on an outdoor grill are magnificent, and grilling lamb chops indoors is just as enjoyable, especially with the crisp-seared exterior and tender, juicy interior that a cast iron grill pan can produce. The Asian-inspired marinade and glaze add beautiful flavor to the natural gamey flavor of the lamb chops. To save time, purchase lamb chops that have already been frenched (cleaned).

FOR THE MARINADE:

1 cup (235 ml) soy sauce

Zest of one orange (reserve ½ (1.5 g) teaspoon for glaze)

1 cup (235 ml) fresh orange juice

1 tablespoon (6 g) chopped fresh ginger

2 tablespoons (28 ml) sesame oil

2 cups (200 g) chopped scallions

1 tablespoon (9 g) red chili flakes

3 garlic cloves (about 3 tablespoons [30 g]), minced

1 tablespoon (18 g) coarse ground black pepper

2 racks New Zealand lamb chops, bones trimmed and then cut into individual chops

FOR CILANTRO MINT GLAZE:

1 tablespoon (20 g) honey

½ teaspoon (1.5 g) orange zest

½ tablespoon (3 g) chopped fresh ginger

¼ cup (15 g) chopped fresh mint

¼ cup (15 g) chopped fresh cilantro

¼ cup (15 g) chopped fresh Italian flat-leaf parsley

½ cup (120 ml) peanut oil

¼ cup (60 ml) rice vinegar

Combine all ingredients for marinade in large mixing bowl and mix well. Place lamb chops in shallow dish and pour marinade over them, covering completely. Cover with plastic wrap and refrigerate for at least 1 hour. Remove from refrigerator 10 minutes prior to grilling.

Combine all ingredients for Cilantro-Mint Glaze, except the oil, in food processor or blender, then blend or pulse to combine. With motor running, gradually add oil in steady stream to emulsify; the mixture should have the consistency of vinaigrette dressing. Remove from blender or processor and place in saucepan. Bring mixture to boil over medium-high heat, then reduce heat and simmer for 15 minutes to thicken.

Spray cast iron stovetop grill pan with nonstick cooking spray and preheat to medium-high heat. Place lamb chops in pan and sear both sides until brown, about 5 minutes on each side. Reduce heat to medium, turn chops, and continue to cook until medium rare, about 3 minutes longer per side. Remove, top with glaze, and serve.

Grilled **Extra-Thick Pork Chops with Molasses-Apple Chutney**

Pork is a great alternative to grilled steak, both for flavor and price. Buying extra thick pork chops with clean bones is a very elegant way to serve grilled chops that look hearty and mouthwatering.

FOR THE MOLASSES-APPLE CHUTNEY:

4 tart green apples, peeled, cored, and rough chopped (about 3 cups [450 g])

1 tablespoon (15 ml) fresh lemon juice

¼ cup (24 g) chopped fresh ginger

½ cup (110 g) light brown sugar, packed

½ cup (75 g) currants

½ cup (75 g) golden raisins

1 yellow onion, chopped

2 tablespoons (300 g) molasses

1 cup (235 ml) cider vinegar

½ cup (120 ml) apple cider

2 tablespoons (28 ml) balsamic vinegar

1 teaspoon (2 g) cinnamon

¼ teaspoon (0.5 g) ground dry mustard

¼ teaspoon (0.5 g) ground cloves

6 peppercorns

4 (1½" [3.5 cm])-thick cleaned (frenched) pork chops

Salt and coarse ground black pepper to taste

FOR THE PORT-APPLE GLAZE:

2 cups (475 ml) apple cider

1 cup (235 ml) ruby port

2 cinnamon sticks

Peel of one orange

2 whole cloves

1 whole star anise

4 whole black peppercorns

1 tablespoon (14 ml) Balsamic Glaze*

Combine all ingredients for chutney in large saucepan and cook over high heat until sugar melts and mixture starts to boil. Stir well, reduce heat to medium, and continue cooking for about 20 minutes, or until chutney appears thick, apples are tender, and onions are translucent.

Combine all ingredients for glaze in saucepan over high heat. Bring to a boil, stir to combine, then reduce heat to medium and cook until reduced to ½ cup (120 ml). Remove from heat, strain glaze through fine sieve, discard spices, add balsamic glaze, and serve warm. If using electric grill pan, preheat to high heat. If using stovetop grill pan, spray with cooking spray and preheat to medium-high heat. Salt and pepper pork chops. Place chops on electric grill, close lid (if there is one), and cook for about 20 minutes, or until chops reach internal temperature of 140°F [60°C]. (Note: the chops may have to be finished in the oven. For the stovetop grill pan, place chops in pan over medium-high heat and cook on one side for 10 minutes or until brown. Turn chops and reduce heat to medium to finish grilling for 10 minutes. Cooking times may vary due to thickness, but chops are done when internal temperature reaches 145°F [65°C]. Let chops stand briefly before serving with warm chutney and drizzled glaze.

*Balsamic glaze is available in most supermarkets where the balsamic vinegar and olive oil is found. If you are unable to find it in your supermarket, simply boil ¼ cup (50 ml) balsamic vinegar with 1 teaspoon (5 g) sugar until reduced to a thick consistency yielding 1 tablespoon (about 15 ml) of glaze.

Grilled **Asian Pork Tenderloin with Fried Bananas and Grilled Polenta**

Pork tenderloin, a tender cut of meat that is perfect for marinating and grilling either indoors or out, makes an inexpensive and tasty meal. This succulent recipe pairs pork tenderloin with fried bananas, grilled polenta, and Vidalia Onion Relish.

2 (1 pound [455 g]) pork tenderloins

½ cup (120 ml) soy sauce

¼ cup (60 ml) orange juice

3 tablespoons (60 g) honey

¼ cup (56 g) packed brown sugar

2 tablespoons (28 ml) Scotch whiskey

3 tablespoons (48 g) hoisin sauce

1 tablespoon (8 g) grated fresh ginger

1 tablespoon (9 g) Chinese five spice powder

1 teaspoon (6 g) salt

2 tablespoons (12 g) coarse ground black pepper

2 tablespoons (28 ml) toasted sesame oil

2 tablespoons (28 ml) vegetable oil plus extra for frying

1 cup (125 g) powdered seafood/vegetable batter, prepared according to package instructions

4 ripe bananas

1 pound (455 g) prepared plain polenta

1 cup (235 ml) Vidalia Onion Relish (recipe follows)

Wash, trim, and dry pork tenderloin, then place in deep dish to marinate. Combine soy sauce, orange juice, honey, brown sugar, whiskey, hoisin sauce, ginger, five spice powder, salt, and pepper in large mixing bowl and whisk to combine. Whisk in sesame and vegetable oils. Pour marinade over pork, then cover and refrigerate for at least 1 hour.

Preheat 4" (10 cm) vegetable oil in saucepan over medium-high heat until oil reaches 365°F (185°C). Preheat electric grill to high heat. Spray stovetop grill pan with nonstick vegetable spray then preheat to high. Prepare batter in mixing bowl according to package instructions. Place pork tenderloin on hot grilling surface and grill for 20 minutes, turning occasionally to brown all sides. The tenderloin is done when the internal temperature reads 130°F (54°C). (Pork tenderloin, unlike pork, should be cooked to only 130°F [55°C] to ensure ideal tenderness.)

Remove tenderloin from grill and set aside to rest for 5 minutes. Slice polenta into ½" (1.5 cm)-thick slices, brush both sides with vegetable oil, and place on hot grill. Grill both sides until golden brown, about 7 minutes per side. Peel bananas and slice ¼" (5 mm)-thick on diagonal. Dip banana

FOR VIDALIA ONION RELISH:

4 slices smoked bacon, chopped

2 large Vidalia onions, chopped

2 cloves garlic (about 2 tablespoons [20 g]), minced

1 teaspoon (1 g) fresh chopped thyme

½ cup (120 ml) dry red wine

½ cup (120 ml) beef broth

2 tablespoons (20 g) honey

2 tablespoons (28 ml) white balsamic vinegar

½ teaspoon (3 g) kosher salt

½ teaspoon (1 g) coarse ground black pepper

slices in batter, coating evenly and thoroughly, and fry in hot oil until golden brown. Place on paper towel to drain, then repeat process to fry remaining bananas. Place grilled polenta on plate, top with sliced pork tenderloin and relish, and serve with fried banana slices.

[For Vidalia Onion Relish]
Fry bacon in skillet over medium-high heat to render fat. When crisp, remove bacon and

reserve for another use. Sauté onions and garlic in bacon fat until tender and translucent, about 5 minutes, then add thyme and sauté for 2 additional minutes. Deglaze pan with red wine, reducing liquid by half, then add beef broth and honey and reduce by half again. Add balsamic vinegar, stir to combine, and season with salt and black pepper. To serve, spoon warm relish over pork tenderloin.

BBQ Grilled **Burgers with Onion-Garlic Jam and Gorgonzola**

Burgers on an indoor grill can be just as good as the outdoor classic, but with an ease that will have you cooking them again and again. Using an electric grill appliance such as the George Foreman grill also reduces the fat, making it a more healthy choice. Selecting toppings and condiments for your burger is a very personal choice, but for this recipe I chose two of my favorites.

FOR THE BURGERS:

2 pounds (905 g) lean ground beef

1 teaspoon (3 g) garlic powder

1 teaspoon (3 g) onion powder

3 dashes hot sauce (optional)

1 teaspoon (2 g) coarse ground black pepper

½ teaspoon (3 g) salt

2 teaspoons (10 ml) Worcestershire sauce

8 hamburger buns

½ cup (125 g) barbecue sauce

16 slices apple or hickory smoked bacon, fried

4 ounces (115 g) crumbled or sliced Gorgonzola cheese

FOR THE ONION-GARLIC JAM:

8 ounces (225 g) Cipollini or pearl onions, chopped

3 cloves (about 3 tablespoons [30 g]) fresh garlic, sliced thin

2 tablespoons (28 g) butter

1 tablespoon (13 g) sugar

½ teaspoon (3 g) salt

½ teaspoon (1 g) fresh cracked black pepper

2 tablespoons (28 ml) water

¼ cup (40 g) honey

¼ teaspoon (0.5 g) ground cinnamon

To make the burgers, combine ground beef, garlic powder, onion powder, hot sauce, black pepper, salt, and Worcestershire sauce in a large mixing bowl and use hands to mix ingredients together. Shape meat mixture into 8 patties, then cover and refrigerate at least 30 minutes. Meanwhile, prepare the onion jam. Melt butter in sauté pan over medium heat, add onions and garlic, and cook until softened, about 4 minutes. Stir in sugar, salt, pepper, and 2 tablespoons water. Reduce heat to low and cook until onions caramelize, about 8 minutes. Transfer onion mixture to food processor fitted with blade attachment, add honey and cinnamon, and purée until slightly chunky. Set aside (jam may be prepared in advance and reheated).

Preheat electric grill to high. Place burgers on grill and cook with lid shut for 7 to 8 minutes, or according to your preference. Toast hamburger buns. Place hamburger patties on bottom half of buns and layer with barbecue sauce, sliced bacon, and blue cheese. Add Onion-Garlic Jam last, followed by top of bun. Serve with french fries or chips.

Grilled **Sirloin with** Smoked-**Pepper Salad and Sherry-Shallot Reduction**

High-quality steaks are, in my opinion, natural for the grill: the high heat sears in the juices and flavors. In this recipe, I've paired a long-standing favorite in my house—grilled steak—with Smoked Pepper Salad for a tremendous combination of flavors. Once smoked, the sweetness of the peppers jump off the plate, pairing perfectly with the Sherry-Shallot Reduction.

4 (6-ounce [168 g]) beef sirloin steaks, about 1" to 1½" (2.5 to 4 cm)-thick

2 teaspoons (4 g) coarse ground black pepper

4 tablespoons (55 g) butter, divided

2 tablespoons (28 ml) olive oil

6 shallots, peeled sliced thin

2 tablespoons (28 g) chopped roasted garlic

1½ cups (355 ml) sherry, divided

4 cups (950 ml) beef broth

1 teaspoon (6 g) kosher salt

2 small yellow onions, peeled, sliced into thin rings, and separated

1 cup (110 g) all-purpose flour

½ teaspoon (3 g) salt

½ teaspoon (1 g) black pepper

Vegetable oil for frying

2 cups (475 ml) Smoked Pepper Salad (recipe follows)

FOR SMOKED PEPPER SALAD:

1 large red pepper

1 large yellow pepper

1 large orange pepper

1 large green pepper

2 large pablaño peppers

1 tablespoon (14 g) hickory or mesquite wood chips

1 tablespoon (14 ml) extra-virgin olive oil

1 tablespoon (14 g) butter

3 cloves (about 3 tablespoons [30 g]) fresh garlic, minced

½ cup (30 g) fresh chopped Italian flat-leaf parsley

½ teaspoon (1 g) paprika

Salt and black pepper to taste

Season each steak with coarse ground black pepper and set aside. Heat olive oil with butter in heavy cast iron skillet over medium heat. Add shallots and sauté until tender, about 4 minutes. Add garlic and sauté an additional 2 minutes until aromatic. Deglaze pan with 1 cup (235 ml) sherry and stir to combine, scraping pan drippings from bottom. Reduce sherry by three quarters, then add beef broth 1 cup (235 ml) at a time to shallot mixture, reducing each time by half. With addition of last cup of beef broth, add remaining cup of sherry. Reduce by one third, then add remaining butter and stir vigorously to incorporate. Season with salt and pepper. Set aside, keeping warm until ready to serve.

Meanwhile, coat cast iron or nonstick grill pan with cooking spray and preheat to high heat. Brush each steak with oil and place on grill pan. Grill until browned, about 7 minutes. Turn, reduce heat to medium, and grill for 7 to 10 additional minutes for medium rare (internal temperature of 125°F [52°C]). Remove from pan and let stand 5 minutes.

Meanwhile, in heavy saucepan or skillet, heat 2" (5 cm) vegetable oil to high heat (about 375°F [190°C]). Combine flour, salt, and black pepper in small bowl and stir with fork to

mix. Toss sliced onions in flour mixture, coating evenly, and transfer to hot oil. Fry until browned, about 4 minutes, then set on paper towels to drain. To serve, place one quarter of sauce on dinner plate, top with grilled sirloin, drizzle with 2 tablespoons (28 ml) additional sauce, and top with pile of fried onion rings. Serve with ½ cup (120 ml) Smoked Pepper Salad (recipe follows).

[For Smoked Pepper Salad]
Wash peppers, remove seeds, core, and slice into ¼" (5 mm)-thick slices. Set aside. Place wood chips in mound in bottom and center of stovetop smoker. Place smoking tray and rack in smoker and spray smoking rack with nonstick cooking spray. Add peppers to smoker in even layer, close lid, and place over medium heat. Smoke peppers for 20 minutes.

Remove from heat and, without opening smoker, let stand for 10 minutes to continue smoking.

Meanwhile, melt butter with olive oil in large sauté pan over high heat. Add garlic and sauté until tender, about 3 minutes. Remove from heat, add smoked peppers, parsley, and paprika. Season with salt and black pepper and toss to incorporate. Keep warm until ready for serving.

2 pounds (905 g) sweet
Italian sausage links

2 cups (475 ml) water

2 (12-ounce [355 ml])
bottles beer

1 bay leaf

3 whole black peppercorns

2 tablespoons (28 g) butter

¼ cup (60 ml) extra-
virgin olive oil, divided

6 cloves (about 6 tablespoons
[60 g]) garlic, sliced thin

2 pounds (905 g) broccoli
rabe, washed and chopped rough

1 teaspoon (6 g) salt

½ teaspoon (1 g) coarse
ground black pepper

1 pound (455 g) cavatappi
pasta, cooked and drained

Parmesan cheese, grated

Sweet Italian Sausage with Garlic and Grilled Broccoli Rabe

I adapted this recipe from a restaurant in Connecticut that serves Broccoli Rabe with Garlic and Italian Sausage. This recipe is a meal in itself!

Bring water, beer, bay leaf, and peppercorns to boil in large saucepan. Place sausage links in boiling mixture and cook for 15 minutes or until firm and opaque. Remove and set aside. If using stovetop grill pan, spray with nonstick cooking spray, coating evenly, and preheat to high heat. If using electric grill, preheat to high heat.

Meanwhile, melt butter with 2 tablespoons (28 ml) olive oil in large sauté pan over medium-high heat. Sauté garlic for 2 minutes, then add broccoli rabe, tossing in oil and butter, and sauté until wilted, about 3 minutes. Add remaining olive oil and pasta and toss to combine. Add salt and pepper and combine. Grill sausage inks until brown and warm throughout, turning to grill all sides, about 5 minutes on each side on stovetop pan and about 10 minutes total on electric grill. To serve, place pasta and broccoli rabe on plates, cut sausage links into equal large chunks, and position on top of pasta. Garnish with freshly grated parmesan cheese.

Grill-**Pressed Pastrami on Rye**

Any New York City deli will probably claim that pastrami on rye is the king of sandwiches, and this recipe is no exception. The key to a great pastrami sandwich is good pastrami with plenty of marbling, and it must be piled high. I have, however, taken a bit of liberty with the mustard in this recipe and created a mouthwatering spread to complement the pile of meat.

¹⁄₄ cup (120 ml) German-style mustard

1 teaspoon (2 g) or more Coleman's dry mustard

1 tablespoon (15 ml) Russian dressing

8 slices good-quality dark rye or pumpernickel bread

12 slices (about ¹⁄₂ pound [225 g]) baby Swiss cheese

2¹⁄₂ pounds (685 g) deli-sliced pastrami

2 tablespoons (30 g) butter, softened

[For Sauce]
In a small bowl, combine the German and dry mustards with the Russian dressing, cover and refrigerate until ready to use.

[To Prepare Dish]
Preheat panini grill to high heat. Lay out four slices of bread, and coat each with a generous amount of mustard spread, reserving half of the spread for later use. Begin layering each sandwich with one slice of Swiss cheese, followed by about ¹⁄₄ pound (115 g) of pastrami, topped with another slice of Swiss cheese, then another ¹⁄₄ pound (115 g) layer of pastrami, finishing with one more slice of Swiss cheese. Divide the remaining mustard spread between the remaining four slices of bread, and place them on top of the sandwiches. Spread the outside of one half of each sandwich with ³⁄₄ teaspoon (1 g) of butter. Place one or two sandwiches on a panini grill, buttered side down, spread another ³⁄₄ teaspoon (1 g) of butter on the other side, close the grill and cook until the bread is browned and the cheese is melted through, about 15 minutes. Repeat with the remaining sandwiches. If using a stovetop grill pan, preheat on medium heat; place the sandwiches in the pan, buttered side down. Cover the sandwiches with a sheet of aluminum foil and weigh them down with a heavy pot or skillet, pressing slightly. Grill these sandwiches until toasted and cheese is melted through, about 8 minutes, then butter the other side, turn the sandwiches over and repeat the cooking process. When using the stovetop grill pan for a sandwich of this thickness, it may be necessary to finish the sandwiches by placing them in an 350°F (180°C) oven long enough to melt the cheese and warm the sandwich all the way through.

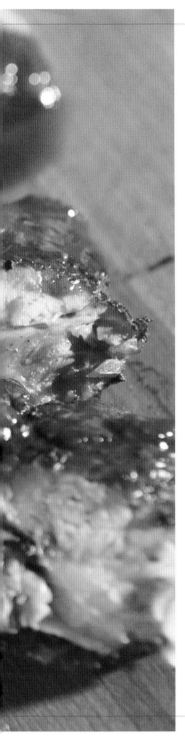

[Makes 4 servings]

Stovetop Smoked **Ribs**

Ribs are one of my favorite grilled foods. Critics might argue there's no other way to enjoy ribs but off an open fire pit, but I beg to disagree. After tasting these moist and delicious ribs, you can decide for yourself.

3 pounds (1.4 kg) pork spareribs

½ cup Sweet Chili Rub (see recipe page 24)

2 tablespoons (28 g) hickory wood chips

1 cup (250 g) Molasses BBQ Schmear (see recipe page 22)

Rub both sides of ribs thoroughly with dry rub, working rub well into ribs. Place wood chips in bottom of stovetop smoker, return drip pan and smoking rack to smoker, and spray smoking rack with nonstick cooking spray. Place ribs on smoking rack and close lid. Place smoker over medium heat and smoke ribs for 45 minutes. Let cool about 15 minutes, then remove from smoker.

Preheat oven to 350°F (180°C). Place ribs in large baking dish, cover thoroughly with Molasses BBQ Schmear, cover, and let stand for 30 minutes. Bake ribs in oven on middle rack, uncovered, for 20 minutes, then set oven to broil and leave ribs on middle rack for 10 minutes, turning once. Remove and serve.

Corn-Smoked **Pork and Chipotle Tacos**

Barbecue pulled pork is a tender and succulent dish when you have several hours to prepare it. This recipe is designed for anyone who doesn't have hours and hours to prepare authentic pulled pork.

FOR THE PORK:

1 (2½-pound [1.0 kg]) bone-in pork butt

Salt and black pepper

1 tablespoon (14 g) corncob wood chips

1 tablespoon (14 g) pecan wood chips

2 tablespoons (28 ml) corn oil

2 large onions, chopped

1½ cups (90 g) chopped fresh cilantro

3 tablespoons (21 g) chopped canned chipotle peppers in adobo sauce

FOR THE TACOS:

12 (5" to 6" [13 to 15 cm]) flour tortillas

Vegetable oil for frying

2 (14.5-ounce [406 ml]) cans black beans, rinsed and drained

1½ cups (150 g) shredded green onions

2 red peppers, thinly sliced

6 ounces (85 g) cheddar cheese, shredded

2 avocados, pitted, peeled, and diced

Prepared salsa

Sour cream

Lime wedges

Season pork generously with salt and pepper. Place wood chips in bottom of stovetop smoker, cover with drip pan and smoking rack, and spray smoking rack with nonstick cooking spray. Position pork butt on cooking rack, cover tightly with heavy-duty aluminum foil, and place smoker over medium heat. Smoke pork for 45 minutes, then remove from heat and let stand, without uncovering, for 10 minutes. Preheat oven to 350°F (180°C), transfer pork to baking dish, and bake on middle rack for 30 minutes, or until internal temperature reaches 165°F (74°C). (The higher temperature ensures the cooked pork will fall off the bone.) Remove pork from oven, let cool, and shred.

Heat corn oil in large skillet over medium-high heat. Add onions and sauté until tender, about 10 minutes. Add shredded pork, cilantro, and chopped chipotle peppers with sauce, stir until heated through, and season with salt and pepper.

Heat vegetable oil in large saucepan over high heat to 375°F (190°C). Wearing oven mitt, use stainless steel kitchen tongs with long handles to grasp flour tortillas one by one between tongs, folding like a taco shell. Dip tortilla in hot oil, fry until golden, then remove and place on paper towels to drain. Repeat with remaining tortillas. Heat beans in saucepan over medium-low heat until warm. Mash beans using fork or potato masher. Arrange tortillas on clean work surface, fill with beans, pork, and shredded green onions, sliced peppers, and shredded cheese, and top with avocados. Serve with salsa, sour cream, and lime wedges.

Unique Utensils

It is said there is someone for everyone. Well, there is a utensil for just about every cooking need as well—some, quite unique. I recently found this great utensil tucked away on a shelf in a kitchen store—taco tongs. Who knew they even existed? It was exactly what I needed for this dish. They simplify the procedure of frying taco shells so any home cook can accomplish it. As utensils go, they are fairly self-explanatory, and, if you can find them, they are quite fun to use.

chapter 5

Poultry

Hickory Smoked Chicken Salad with Cheese Toasts

Hickory smoking the chicken for this salad lends a bold flavor to a very popular dish.

FOR THE CHICKEN:

4 (6-ounce [168 g]) boneless, skinless chicken breasts

Salt and black pepper to taste

1 tablespoon (14 g) pecan wood chips

1 tablespoon (14 g) hickory wood chips

1 cup (125 g) pecans, chopped

1 bunch green onions, chopped

3 slices wood-smoked bacon, cooked and chopped

1 (4.5-ounce [127 g]) can chopped green chilies, drained

2 tablespoons (8 g) chopped fresh Italian flat-leaf parsley

1 medium red pepper, diced

½ cup (75 g) dried cranberries, chopped

FOR THE DRESSING:

1 cup (225 g) mayonnaise

2 tablespoons (28 ml) cider vinegar

¼ teaspoon (0.3 g) ground nutmeg

1 tablespoon (15 g) honey mustard

1 tablespoon (15 ml) lemon juice

1 tablespoon (15 ml) orange juice

½ teaspoon (3 g) salt

½ teaspoon (1 g) black pepper

FOR THE CHEESE TOASTS:

Makes 8 wedges

4 slices thin white sandwich bread, crusts removed

2 tablespoons (28 ml) olive oil

4 ounces (58 g) herbed Boursin or goat cheese, softened

1 tablespoon (4 g) minced fresh chives

Coarse ground black pepper

Place wood chips in bottom of stovetop smoker, return drip pan and smoking rack to smoker, and spray rack with nonstick cooking spray. Season chicken breasts with salt and pepper, place in smoker, cover, and smoke over medium heat for 30 minutes. Remove from heat and let stand for 15 minutes. Remove cover of smoker, transfer chicken to cutting board, and shred into thin strips. Cover and refrigerate for at least 1 hour or until completely cool.

Combine all the ingredients for dressing in mixing bowl and stir. Cover and chill for at least 30 minutes. Combine chicken with pecans, green onions, bacon, green chilies, parsley, red pepper, and cranberries in large mixing bowl. Top with dressing, stir to combine, cover, and refrigerate until cold throughout. Serve on bed of greens or as sandwich on a toasted croissant.

For the cheese toasts, preheat stovetop grill pan or electric grill to high heat. Brush both sides of bread with olive oil and grill until golden on both sides, about 5 minutes per side. Remove and set aside to cool. Meanwhile, combine cheese with ½ teaspoon (1 g) black pepper and chives. Preheat broiler to high heat, spread cheese mixture on one side of each piece of toast, and broil until cheese begins to melt and turn golden brown. Remove, cut into triangles, and serve with chicken salad.

Pulled Smoked Chicken with Pan-Roasted Fennel, Tomato, and Soft Polenta

Smoking a chicken is a great way to concentrate the flavors while also sealing in the bird's natural juices. I pair this recipe for smoked chicken with simple pan-roasted vegetables for a great meal.

1 whole roaster chicken, cleaned and quartered

2 teaspoons (12 g) salt

2 teaspoons (4 g) freshly ground black pepper

1 teaspoon (2 g) cayenne pepper

2 tablespoons (28 g) apple wood chips

1 tablespoon (14 g) oak wood chips

3/4 cup (175 ml) olive oil

1 red onion, cut in half and sliced thin

2 bulbs fennel, sliced thin

3 cloves (about 3 tablespoons [30 g]) garlic, sliced thin

1 pint (200 g) grape orchery tomatoes, washed and patted dry

Soft Polenta (recipe follows)

FOR SOFT POLENTA:

6 cups (1.4 l) chicken or vegetable stock

1/4 cup (55 g) butter

1 teaspoon (6 g) salt

1 1/2 cups (250 g) quick-cooking polenta

1 cup (80 g) freshly grated parmesan cheese

1/2 cup (120 g) mascarpone cheese

1/2 teaspoon (1 g) freshly ground black pepper

Prepare a stovetop smoker by placing the apple and oak wood chips in bottom of smoker, return the drip tray and food tray to the smoker, and spray rack with nonstick cooking spray. Combine salt, pepper, and cayenne pepper in small bowl, then rub chicken pieces thoroughly with spice mixture.

Heat 1/2 cup (120 ml) olive oil in large, oven-proof skillet over medium-high heat, add chicken, and sear or brown on all sides, about 8 minutes, turning each piece once. Remove chicken and position in single layer on smoking rack of smoker. Close lid and smoke over medium heat for 45 minutes.

Preheat oven to 350°F (180°C). Meanwhile, using same skillet, add remaining olive oil, heat over medium-high heat, and sauté onion and fennel for 4 minutes or just until fennel becomes tender. Add garlic and tomatoes and place in hot oven to roast for 20 minutes. Remove chicken from smoker, transfer to cutting board, and shred into thin strips. Serve with roasted vegetables over soft polenta, drizzled with pan drippings.

[For Soft Polenta]
Bring stock, butter, and salt to a boil in large heavy saucepan. Gradually whisk in polenta. Reduce heat to medium-low, stirring constantly, until polenta thickens, about 5 minutes. Remove from heat, add parmesan cheese, mascarpone cheese, and black pepper, stir vigorously to incorporate, and serve.

[Makes 6 servings]

Asian-Inspired Tea-Smoked Duck

The Asian influence on American cooking is a wonderful phenomenon as Asian flavorings, oils, vinegars, and spices bring tremendous flavor and texture to American food. Smoking poultry using tea leaves and raw rice is an Asian specialty that imparts subtle, yet powerful, flavor on chicken, pheasant, quail, or duck.

6 duck breasts, about 2 pounds (1 kg)

3 cups (585 g) cooked white rice

FOR THE MARINADE:

$\frac{1}{2}$ cup (120 ml) maple syrup

$\frac{1}{2}$ cup (120 ml) chicken broth

$\frac{1}{2}$ cup (120 ml) orange juice

$\frac{1}{2}$ cup (120 ml) apple cider

$\frac{1}{2}$ cup (120 ml) water

$\frac{1}{2}$ cup (75 g) brown sugar

1 teaspoon (3 g) ground
Szechwan peppercorns

1 tablespoon (18 g) salt

1 teaspoon (3 g) five-spice powder

SMOKING MIXTURE:

2 tablespoons (28 g)
mesquite wood chips

$\frac{1}{2}$ cup (30 g) black tea leaves

$\frac{1}{2}$ cup (75 g) brown sugar

$\frac{1}{2}$ cup (98 g) raw rice

3 strips orange zest

2 tablespoons (28 ml) sesame oil

FOR ORANGE AND FENNEL GLAZE:

Makes about 1 cup (250 ml)

1 tablespoon (14 ml) olive oil

1 red onion, chopped

1 cup (100 g) chopped fresh fennel

$\frac{1}{2}$ cup (160 g) orange marmalade

$\frac{1}{4}$ cup (60 ml) white
balsamic vinegar

Salt and freshly ground
black pepper

Wash duck breasts, pat dry, and place in deep baking dish. Combine all ingredients for marinade in large mixing bowl and stir together. Pour over duck breasts, cover, and refrigerate overnight or for at least 8 hours. Combine ingredients for smoking mixture in large mixing bowl and set aside. Remove duck from marinade and pat dry. Fill lower part of steamer with enough water to come within 1 inch (2.5 cm) of cooking rack. Bring water to rolling boil, place duck on rack, and steam the duck for 30 minutes, keeping water at boil and replenishing it as it boils away.

Prepare a stovetop smoker with the smoking mixture placed in the bottom. Return the drip tray and food rack to the smoker. Place duck breasts on rack, skin side down. Cover the smoker and place over medium heat. Smoke duck for 30 minutes, then turn off heat and let stand for 5 minutes while smoke subsides. The duck should be a rich golden brown with an internal temperature of at least 165°F (74°C). Serve duck over white rice topped with orange glaze.

[For Orange and Fennel Glaze]
Heat olive oil over medium-high heat in heavy skillet. Add onion and fennel, then sauté until tender and onion is translucent. Add orange marmalade and balsamic vinegar, stir, and heat through to thicken. Remove from heat and serve warm.

Smoked **Stuffed Turkey Breast**

Don't save stuffed turkey breast for just the holidays—with this recipe you can prepare and enjoy it any time of the year. Readily available, cleaned, and ready to cook, boneless turkey breast makes an excellent, healthy alternative for dinner. Making homemade stuffing is a simple process that requires only a few ingredients, but if you are pressed for time, it's possible to purchase stuffed turkey breasts in most supermarkets.

1 (4-pound [(2 kg]) whole boneless turkey breast

2 ounces (55 g) pancetta, sliced thick, diced

1 cup (220 g) ground chorizo or sweet Italian sausage

1 yellow onion, chopped

3 cloves (about 3 tablespoons [30 g]) garlic, minced

1 large Granny Smith apple, peeled, cored, and chopped

4 tablespoons (55 g) butter, plus 2 tablespoons (28 g) for gravy

1 (16-ounce [275 g]) package seasoned cornbread or bread stuffing mix

2 tablespoons (16 g) all-purpose flour

1 cup (235 ml) chicken broth

2 cups (475 ml) milk

Salt and black pepper to taste

3 tablespoons (42 g) maple wood chips

Wash and pat dry turkey breast, season with salt and pepper, and set aside. Cook pancetta in large skillet over medium-high heat until crisp, about 10 minutes. Remove pancetta and place in mixing bowl. Add chorizo or Italian sausage, onion, and garlic to skillet.

Cook until sausage is brown and onion is tender and translucent, about 7 minutes, then add apple, stir to combine, and cook for 2 additional minutes. Remove from heat and transfer to bowl with pancetta.

Melt 4 tablespoons (55 g) butter in same skillet over medium heat, add stuffing mix, and toast stuffing coating thoroughly with the butter, for 5 minutes. Combine with sausage mixture. Melt remaining butter in hot skillet, stirring to scrape up pan drippings. Sprinkle with flour and whisk to combine, then cook flour (roux) until toasty brown, taking care not to let it burn.

Gradually add milk ¼ cup (60 ml) at a time, stirring vigorously to prevent lumping. Bring gravy to boil, then reduce to simmer and cook for 5 minutes. Season with salt and black pepper and set aside, keeping gravy warm until ready to serve.

Add chicken broth to stuffing mixture and stir to combine. Spread turkey breast open and layer with stuffing mixture, then gather turkey breast up, wrapping it around stuffing. Tie turkey breast closed using kitchen twine.

Place wood chips in bottom of stovetop smoker, return drip pan and smoking rack to smoker, and spray smoking rack with nonstick cooking spray. Position turkey breast on rack, cover, place smoker over medium heat, and smoke turkey for 1½ hours or until breast reaches internal temperature of 165°F (74°C). To check temperature, open lid to smoker very slightly and quickly pierce thermometer into breast 3" (7.5 cm) until temperature registers. If turkey breast sits to close to smoker, cover smoker tightly using heavy-duty aluminum foil, sealing around edges of base of smoker.

Remove smoker from heat after 1½ hours and let stand 10 minutes. Remove lid and place turkey breast on cutting board. Remove twine and slice breast. Serve with mashed potatoes and pan gravy.

[Makes 4 servings]

Smoked **Chicken with Pasta and Marinated Mozzarella**

I recently discovered that tossing bocconcini mozzarella into a sauce just before it's complete is a great way to soften the cheese while maintaining its shape and bite. I love using fresh mozzarella cheese this way because it adds a subtle flavor but hearty texture to the dish. If you can't find bocconcini mozzarella, simply purchase a large block of buffalo mozzarella and cut it into chunks.

1 tablespoon (14 g) apple wood chips

4 (6-ounce [168 g]) boneless, skinless chicken breasts

Salt and black pepper to taste

3 tablespoons (42 ml) olive oil

4 ounces (115 g) pancetta, diced

2 tablespoons (20 g) chopped garlic

1 cup (235 ml) white wine

3 tablespoons (42 g) butter

¼ cup (15 g) fresh basil, torn

1 pound (455 g) marinated bocconcini mozzarella*, drained

1 pound (455 g) penne pasta, cooked, drained, and kept warm

Place apple wood chips in bottom of stovetop smoker, return drip pan and smoking rack to smoker, and spray rack with nonstick cooking spray. Season chicken breasts with salt and black pepper, place in smoker, cover, and smoke over medium heat for 30 minutes. Remove from heat and let stand for 15 minutes. Cook pancetta in large skillet over medium-high heat about 7 minutes until fat is rendered and pancetta is crisp. Remove pancetta and set aside, reserving fat in pan. Add olive oil to pan and heat, then add garlic and sauté for 2 minutes. Deglaze pan with white wine, reducing by one quarter, then whisk in butter.

Add pancetta, smoked chicken, fresh basil, and mozzarella cheese to pan.

Remove from heat, stirring gradually to soften mozzarella cheese. When strings begin to form from mozzarella, pour mixture over pasta and serve.

*Bocconcini (bohk-kohn-CHEE-nee) mozzarella refers to small nuggets (about 1 inch [2.5 cm] in diameter) of fresh mozzarella. Generally, they are sold packed in whey or water, but many supermarket delis also sell them marinated in olive oil, basil, and sun-dried tomatoes. If you can only find them packed in water, toss mozzarella with ¼ cup (60 ml) extra-virgin olive oil, ¼ cup (15 g) chopped fresh basil, and 3 tablespoons (42 g) chopped sun-dried tomatoes. Cover and refrigerate for at least 1 hour.

Roasted **Chicken Panini on Jalapeño Cheddar Bread**

When visiting home in the south, jalapeño cheddar bread is one of my favorite indulgences. I have developed these sandwiches using my own Jalapeño Cheddar Bread that works perfectly for a panini. Even if you are skipping the sandwich part, toasted jalapeño cheddar bread is great on its own.

8 slices jalapeño-cheddar bread

2 tablespoons (28 g) butter

¼ pound (115 g) sliced provolone cheese

¼ pound (115 g) sliced cheddar cheese

1 pound (455 g) deli-roasted chicken breast, sliced thin

4 teaspoons (20 g) Dijon mustard

4 teaspoons (20 g) Chipotle Ketchup (recipe follows)

8 slices apple smoked bacon, cooked

FOR CHIPOTLE KETCHUP:

1 cup (240 g) ketchup

¼ cup (56 g) chili sauce

3 tablespoons (42 ml) chipotle pepper hot sauce*

½ teaspoon (1 g) onion powder

½ teaspoon (1 g) garlic powder

½ teaspoon (1 g) chili powder

1 teaspoon (5 ml) red wine vinegar

Preheat electric panini grill to medium-high heat. If using stovetop grill pan, spray pan with nonstick cooking spray and then preheat to medium-high heat. Butter one side of four slices of bread and place on hot grill, buttered side down. (If you cannot prepare all four sandwiches at once, cook in batches until complete, keeping grilled sandwiches wrapped or in warm oven).

Spread Chipotle Ketchup on bread, reserving some for top slice of bread. Layer on provolone cheese and cheddar cheese, dividing evenly among four slices of bread. Spread remaining Chipotle Ketchup over second slice of bread, place on top of sandwich, spread side down, and butter top of sandwich. If using panini grill, close lid and press firmly, then grill sandwich for about 10 minutes or until cheese is melted and bread is well toasted. If using stovetop grill pan, spray a small piece of aluminum foil with nonstick cooking spray and place spray side down on top of sandwich. Press sandwich into hot skillet using bacon press or heavy skillet. Toast on one side for about 4 minutes, or until bread is toasted and cheese begins to melt. Flip sandwiches over and repeat process. Remove sandwiches from cooking appliance and while still hot, taking care not to burn fingers, pull sandwiches apart. Insert sliced chicken and bacon, dividing both evenly between all four sandwiches. Spread mustard on other side and close sandwich. Cut in half and serve hot.

[For Chipotle Ketchup]
Combine all ingredients in bowl and stir to mix together. Cover and refrigerate for at least one hour. Serve as a condiment on sandwiches or as a marinade ingredient for grilled meats and poultry.

*Chipotle pepper sauce is available in the international food section of most supermarkets. One brand I recommend is Goya.

Whole Grain Mustard- and Bourbon-Grilled Chicken

Whole-grain mustard and bourbon are two ingredients made for each other. As a marinade, and then a basting sauce, the sweet, tangy combination imparts a delicious flavor on chicken, creating a caramelized "crust" during grilling. Enjoy with your favorite grilled vegetables or the Smoked Corn on the Cob on page 105.

4 (6-ounce [168 g]) boneless, skinless chicken breasts

1 cup (235 ml) fresh orange juice

½ cup (120 ml) bourbon

¼ cup (60 g) whole grain mustard

2 tablespoons (20 g) honey

2 tablespoons (28 g) packed brown sugar

2 tablespoons (28 ml) soy sauce

1 tablespoon (6 g) coarse ground black pepper

¼ teaspoon (0.5 g) ground nutmeg

¼ teaspoon (0.5 g) ground cloves

Combine orange juice, bourbon, whole grain mustard, honey, brown sugar, and soy sauce in heavy saucepan, bring to boil for 1 minute, then reduce to simmer. Add nutmeg and cloves. Cook for an additional 10 minutes or until sauce is dark and thick. Remove and let cool completely.

Using half of sauce, coat chicken breasts thoroughly, then place in baking dish large enough to accommodate breasts in single layer. Sprinkle evenly with black pepper, cover, and refrigerate for at least 1 hour. Preheat stovetop grill pan or electric grill to high heat. If using stove top pan, spray with nonstick cooking spray. Grill chicken until brown and cooked through, about 10 minutes on each side or 15 minutes total in electric grill pan with lid. Serve with your favorite grilled vegetables and potatoes.

Skillet Chicken Fajitas with Three Peppers

In southwestern cooking, fajitas are a staple. Large stovetop grill pans work well for this type of meal because everything can be prepared in the same pan. For this recipe, I used a large, rectangular cast iron grill pan (often sold as reversible pans, with a griddle on the other side), but you could also prepare this meal in individual cast-iron fajita pans.

1½ pounds (680 g) boneless, skinless chicken breasts, sliced thin

1 tablespoon (14 ml) vegetable oil

2 poblaño chili peppers, roasted and sliced thin

Olive oil

1 small yellow onion, sliced thin

1 red pepper, sliced thin

1 yellow pepper, sliced thin

½ cup (65 g) fresh or frozen corn kernels

12 flour tortillas

¼ cup (15 g) fresh cilantro leaves, chopped

6 ounces (85 g) shredded cheddar cheese

¼ cup (58 g) sour cream

2 avocados, sliced thin

Vegetable oil spray

FOR FAJITA SEASONING BLEND:

2 tablespoons (18 g) ancho chili powder

2 teaspoons (6 g) garlic powder

2 teaspoons (6 g) coriander

2 teaspoons (6 g) dried oregano

1 teaspoon (3 g) ground cumin

½ teaspoon (3 g) salt

½ teaspoon (1 g) black pepper

Combine all ingredients for fajita seasoning in small bowl and mix thoroughly. Toss sliced chicken breast with fajita seasoning blend and vegetable oil, using hands to massage chicken meat and thoroughly coat with seasonings. Cover and refrigerate seasoned chicken for at least 1 hour and up to overnight.

To roast poblaño pepper, coat with olive oil and place under broiler; grill until charred black on all sides, then remove and place in brown paper bag to "sweat" off skin. Remove pepper from bag, pull off charred skin, remove white veins and seeds from inside, slice flesh thinly, and set aside.

Preheat oven to 200°F (93°C). Stack and wrap flour tortillas in aluminum foil and place in oven to warm until ready to serve. Spray stovetop grill pan with vegetable spray and preheat over high heat. Add chicken, cooking on all sides until brown and cooked through, about 20 minutes. After 10 minutes of cooking chicken, move to one side of grill pan and place red and yellow peppers, corn kernels, and onion on other side. Cook until brown and tender, about 10 minutes. Remove pan from heat, add poblaño peppers to pepper and onion mixture, and serve hot from the pan. Remove flour tortillas from oven and serve warm. Serve fajitas with shredded cheddar cheese, cilantro leaves, sour cream, and sliced avocado.

Skillet-Grilled Chicken with Monchego, Cheddar, and Onions

One-dish cooking is a great way to pull together a hearty meal without a big mess. The size of your skillet dictates how much you can cook in one pan. Choose a large, oven-proof skillet that is a least 12" (30 cm) wide to accommodate all this recipe offers.

4 (6-ounce [168 g]) boneless, skinless chicken breasts

¼ cup (25 g) Spicy Dry Rub (see recipe page 29)

¼ cup (63 g) Dark Ale Grilling Sauce (see recipe page 24)

4 tablespoons (60 ml) vegetable oil

1 large yellow onion, sliced

1 red pepper, seeded, thinly sliced

1 yellow pepper, seeded, thinly sliced

3 cloves (about 3 tablespoons [30 g]) garlic, minced

2 tablespoons (8 g) chopped fresh cilantro

Salt and black pepper

6 ounces (112 g) shredded Monchego cheese

6 ounces (168 g) shredded cheddar cheese

2 large carrots, peeled and chopped

2 cups (140 g) broccoli florets

2 tablespoons (28 g) butter

Place chicken breasts in shallow pan large enough to hold all four at once. Rub all sides of chicken with dry rub, coating thoroughly. Cover and refrigerate for at least 4 hours and up to overnight. Place a steam basket in the bottom of a large sauce pot, and add enough water to the pot so it just reaches the bottom of the basket. Heat water over high heat. Place carrots and broccoli in steam basket, and steam until tender, but not soft, about 10 minutes. Remove vegetables and set aside.

Remove chicken and brush generously with Dark Ale Grilling Sauce. Preheat large cast iron grill pan over medium-high heat. Spray grill pan with nonstick cooking spray. Toss sliced onion and peppers in 2 tablespoons (28 ml) vegetable oil and grill until tender and brown on both sides, about 10 minutes. Remove, transfer to bowl, and toss with garlic and cilantro. Preheat oven broiler. Add remaining oil to grill pan and grill chicken for 10 minutes on one side. Turn chicken, add steamed vegetables to pan, top with butter, and season with salt and pepper. Top chicken with onion and garlic mixture, then spread equal amounts Monchego and cheddar cheeses evenly over chicken breasts. Place dish under broiler and cook until cheese is melted and bubbling, about 5 minutes. Remove and serve chicken alongside grilled vegetables.

Seafood

Banana Leaf–Smoked **Monkfish** with Coconut-Cilantro Pesto

Monkfish is often called "poor man's lobster" because of its lobsterlike sweetness and texture. Yet that firm, stable texture also holds up well for smoking and grilling. In this recipe, the banana leaf enclosure helps capture flavors and moistness.

FOR COCONUT-CILANTRO PESTO:

1 cup (60 g) fresh cilantro leaves

½ cup (30 g) fresh basil leaves

¼ cup (28 g) unsweetened dried coconut flakes

2 cloves (about 2 tablespoons [20 g]) fresh garlic, peeled

¼ teaspoon (0.7 g) curry powder

1 tablespoon (15 g) packed brown sugar

¼ cup (60 ml) coconut milk

½ cup (120 ml) olive oil

Salt and black pepper to taste

---

4 (6-ounce [168 g]) monkfish steaks

3 tablespoons (18 g) Spicy Dry Rub (see recipe page 24)

2 banana leaves

1 tablespoon (14 g) oak wood chips

1 tablespoon (14 g) pecan wood chips

1½ tablespoons (21 ml) sesame oil

1½ pounds (680 g) crimini mushrooms, brushed clean

3 cloves (about 3 tablespoons [30 g]) garlic, minced

2 tablespoons (28 ml) peanut oil

1 tablespoon (14 g) butter

1 cup (235 ml) Coconut-Cilantro Pesto (recipe follows)

Rub fish steaks evenly with 2 tablespoons (12 g) dry rub. Working on a flat surface, trim banana leaves into 12" x 8" (30 x 20 cm) rectangles. With the banana leaf in front of you, place the monkfish steak in the middle, drizzle sesame oil onto the fish, fold banana leaf over onto steak, and then fold in the sides, rolling the pouch away from you, forming a sealed package. Tear ½" (1.2 cm)-wide strips from additional leaves and use them as ribbon to tie the packages closed.

Mix wood chips and place in center of bottom of smoker. Return drip tray to smoker, fill with ½ cup (120 ml) water, return smoking rack to smoker, and place monkfish pouches in smoker. Cover, place over medium heat, and smoke monkfish for 30 minutes. Remove and let stand, covered, for 10 minutes.

Meanwhile, heat peanut oil with butter in large skillet over medium-high heat, then add mushrooms and garlic and sauté until tender and brown, about 10 minutes. Season with remaining tablespoon of Spicy Dry Rub, cook for 2 minutes, and set aside. Remove fish steaks from smoker, and open banana leaf to expose fish. To serve, top with Coconut-Cilantro Pesto and sautéed mushrooms.

Combine cilantro, basil, coconut, garlic, curry powder, and brown sugar in bowl of food processor fitted with blade attachment. Pulse to chop herbs, then add coconut milk, and pulse to puree. With processor running, add olive oil in steady stream to emulsify. Remove, season with salt and black pepper, and refrigerate in airtight container until ready to use. Pesto can be made ahead of time and stored up to 4 days or frozen in airtight container for up to 1 month. Before serving, allow pesto to come to room temperature.

Smoked **Salmon and Potato Pie**

My friend Cliff cooks salmon pie for me time and time again, but wouldn't think of sharing the recipe. So I created my own! I would assume it can't compare to his mother's vintage recipe, but I gave it a good effort, including smoking the salmon, which intensifies the flavor.

FOR CRUST:

1 1/3 cups (147 g) all-purpose flour

1/3 cup (46 g) fine yellow cornmeal

1/2 teaspoon (3 g) salt

1/2 cup (57 g) shredded yellow Cheddar cheese

1/3 cup (75 g) cold butter, cut into pieces

1/3 cup (75 g) shortening

5 tablespoons (70 ml) ice water

2 tablespoons (28 g) alder wood chips

3/4 pound (0.3 kg) salmon fillet

1/2 teaspoon (3 g) kosher salt

1 teaspoon (2 g) coarsely ground black pepper

1 tablespoon (14 ml) olive oil

1 tablespoon (14 g) butter

1 cup (120 g) thinly sliced leeks

1 medium Vidalia onion, thinly sliced

1/2 (57 g) cup shredded white cheddar cheese

2 cups (220 g) shredded Yukon Gold potatoes (grated on large grate of box grater)

2 tablespoons (8 g) chopped fresh basil

1/8 teaspoon (0.3 g) cayenne pepper

1 cup (235 ml) half-and-half

2 eggs

1 egg yolk

For the crust, add the flour, cornmeal, and salt in the bowl of a food processor fitted with the blade attachment, pulsing three or four times until combined. Add cheese, butter, and shortening, and pulse five or six times or until crumbly. With processor running, gradually add the water, and process until dough forms a ball and separates from the sides of the bowl, adding more water 1 tablespoon (15 ml) at a time, if necessary. Remove dough from bowl, and gather into two equally sized balls, wrap each ball in plastic wrap and chill for 1 hour.

Prepare the stovetop smoker with alder wood chips in the bottom, return the drip tray and food rack to the smoker and spray with nonstick cooking spray. Season the salmon fillet with salt and pepper, place on the food rack of the smoker, cover and place over medium heat. Smoke the salmon for 30 minutes. Remove from heat and let stand, uncovered, for 5 additional minutes. Set salmon aside to cool. Meanwhile, sauté the leeks and onions in butter and olive oil over medium-high heat for 10 minutes, or until tender. Transfer to a large bowl, stir in smoked salmon (breaking it up as you stir), cheese, potatoes, basil, and cayenne pepper.

Whisk half and half and eggs in small bowl, then season with salt and pepper. Add egg mixture to salmon mixture, stir to combine, and set aside. Remove dough from refrigerator, and working with one ball at a time, roll dough on lightly floured surface into 1/8" (3 mm)-thick and 14" (35 cm)-wide circle. Place one dough round into bottom of 9" (23 cm) pie plate with 2" (5 cm) high sides. Spoon salmon mixture into pie plate and top with second dough round. Using fingers, pinch two crusts together around perimeter of pie plate, crimping dough into scalloped pattern. Cut six small slits in dough to vent. Bake at 450°F [230°C] for 10 minutes. Reduce heat to 350°F [180°C] and bake for 40 additional minutes or until golden brown. Remove and let stand for 10 minutes, then slice and serve.

Grilled **Seafood Salad**

The combination of flavors and textures in this salad make a great summer treat. This recipe combines tender shrimp, large scallops, crab, and lobster in a delicious creamy dressing. Enjoy ice cold as a side dish or between two slices of crusty bread as a hearty sandwich.

2 pounds (905 g) large shrimp, peeled and deveined

2 pounds (905 g) large scallops

1/4 cup (60 ml) olive oil

1/2 teaspoon (3 g) kosher salt

1 teaspoon (2 g) fresh cracked black pepper

1/2 pound (225 g) lump crabmeat

1/2 pound (225 g) cooked lobster meat

3 sliced scallions (greens and whites)

1 red pepper, diced

2 stalks celery, diced (optional)

1/4 cup (15 g) chopped fresh Italian flat-leaf parsley

2 tablespoons (8 g) chopped fresh tarragon

1 cup (225 g) mayonnaise

1/4 cup (58 g) sour cream

1 tablespoon (15 g) Dijon mustard

1 tablespoon (14 ml) olive oil

1 tablespoon (14 ml) cider vinegar

1 teaspoon (5 ml) lemon juice

1/2 teaspoon (0.6 g) red pepper flakes

2 cloves (about 2 tablespoons [20 g]) garlic, minced

2 tablespoons (8 g) minced fresh chives

10 ounces (30 g) mixed salad greens, such as mesclun mix or baby spinach

Toss shrimp, scallops, and calamari with olive oil in large mixing bowl and season with salt and pepper. Preheat stovetop grill pan or electric grill to high heat. If using the stovetop grill, spray with nonstick cooking spray before preheating. Place shrimp and scallops on grill in batches and grill until cooked through on both sides. (Cooking times will vary depending on cooking appliance. If using the stovetop grill pan, cook shrimp and scallops for 5 minutes on each side or until golden. If using an electric grill cook for about 10 minutes, about 5 minutes on each side. Remove shrimp and scallops and set aside to cool.

Combine crabmeat, lobster, scallions, red pepper, celery, parsley, and tarragon in mixing bowl. Add mayonnaise, sour cream, Dijon mustard, olive oil, cider vinegar, lemon juice, garlic, and chives to a separate bowl and whisk to combine. Add shrimp and scallops to bowl with crab and lobster, pour on dressing, and toss to thoroughly coat. Cover and refrigerate for at least 2 hours, or until completely cold. Serve cold over a bed of mixed salad greens.

Smoked **Oysters with Spicy Tomato Mignonette**

Oysters are one of the few foods that can be enjoyed cooked or raw. Oysters on the half shell are an easy treat with many healthful benefits. Smoking the oysters intensifies their flavor and imparts a rich, smoky taste. This recipe pairs smoked oysters with a spicy tomato mignonette, but don't overdo the mignonette or it will distract from the oyster's natural flavors.

16 oysters, shucked in half, juices and meat intact

2 slices bacon, cut into 16 pieces

Fresh cracked black pepper to taste

2 tablespoons (28 g) alder wood chips

1 cup (235 ml) Spicy Tomato Mignonette (recipe follows)

Place alder chips in bottom of smoker. Sprinkle each oyster with black pepper and top with piece of bacon. Place oysters in smoker and smoke over medium heat for 20 minutes. Remove from smoker and serve with Spicy Tomato Mignonette.

FOR SPICY TOMATO MIGNONETTE:

2 tablespoons (12 g) minced fresh ginger

1 jalapeño or serrano chilie, seeded and minced

1/4 cup (25 g) chopped scallions, including green parts

1 cup (150 g) chopped red tomato

1/2 cup (75 g) chopped yellow tomato

Juice of 1 lime

Zest of 1 lime

1 tablespoon (14 ml) white balsamic vinegar

1 teaspoon (5 ml) sesame oil

1 teaspoon (2 g) fresh cracked black pepper

Salt to taste

Combine all ingredients in bowl and stir. Cover and refrigerate for at least one hour. The mignonette can be refrigerated in an airtight container for up to 4 days.

Grilled **Honey Pepper Scallops with Wild Rice Risotto**

I think scallops are one of the best gifts of the sea, and when grilled, their flavor really intensifies. This recipe, which uses a simple marinade and seasonings, makes an easy dinner for any night of the week. Serve with a side of hearty risotto.

16 jumbo sea scallops

1 cup (235 ml) soy sauce

1/4 cup (60 ml) balsamic vinegar

1/4 cup (80 g) honey

2 tablespoons (12 g) freshly
minced ginger

3 cloves (about 3 tablespoons
[30 g]) garlic, minced

1/2 teaspoon (3 g) kosher salt

1 tablespoon (6 g) coarse ground
black pepper

FOR WILD RICE RISOTTO:

5 to 7 cups (1,175 to 1,645 ml)
chicken or vegetable stock

2 tablespoons (28 ml) olive oil

3 shallots, finely chopped

2 cloves (about 2 tablespoons
[20 g]) garlic, minced

2 cups (390 g) Arborio rice

1 cup (235 ml) dry white vermouth
or dry white wine

1 cup (165 g) wild rice, cooked

2 tablespoons (28 g) butter

1/4 cup (20 g) freshly grated
parmesan cheese

Salt and freshly ground
black pepper

2 tablespoons (28 ml) olive oil

2 tablespoons (28 g) butter

1 pound (455 g) large
asparagus spears

1 red pepper, seeded and very
thinly sliced

1 yellow pepper, seeded and very
thinly sliced

1/2 cup (50 g) thinly sliced
shitake mushrooms

1/4 teaspoon (0.6 g) cayenne pepper

Combine soy sauce with balsamic vinegar, honey, ginger, garlic, and salt in large mixing bowl. Add scallops, toss gently to coat, then cover and refrigerate for at least 1 hour and up to 2 hours.

Meanwhile, heat stock in large saucepot. In separate large pot or skillet, heat olive oil over medium heat. Sauté shallots and garlic for about 3 minutes or until tender. Add rice and increase heat to medium-high, stirring rice to coat evenly with oil so it begins to turn translucent. Add vermouth and stir to combine. When vermouth is absorbed, add one ladle stock, salt, and pepper and stir until rice absorbs stock. Continue adding ladles of stock, stirring and allowing stock to be absorbed before adding next. (This entire process should take about 20 minutes.) Continue adding stock and stirring until rice is soft but with a slight bite. With last addition of stock add wild rice, then stir to incorporate. Remove from heat, add butter and parmesan cheese, and season with salt and pepper if needed.

Peel outside skin from asparagus spears and break away tough ends, then slice spears thinly lengthwise. Heat 2 tablespoons (28 ml) olive oil in large skillet over medium-high heat. Sauté asparagus with peppers and mushrooms, season with salt, pepper, and cayenne, then set aside, keeping warm. Preheat stovetop grill pan or electric grill to high heat. Remove scallops from marinade, draining well, then sprinkle evenly with black pepper. Spray grill with nonstick cooking spray, place scallops on grill and cook for about 5 minutes per side, turning only once. (Scallops cook fast and when done will be opaque and tender in the middle). Remove scallops from the grill, let stand 3 minutes and serve along side the Wild Rice Risotto and sautéed asparagus.

Smoked **Salmon Fillet with Peas and Pancetta over Pasta**

Smoked salmon has a very unique flavor that complements a simple sauce of peas and pancetta over pasta.

1 pound (455 g) ribbon pasta (either fettuccini, linguini, or parpradelle)

1 teaspoon (2.3 g) cumin seed

1 teaspoon (2.3 g) fennel seed

2 teaspoons (4 g) coarse cracked black pepper

1 teaspoon (5 g) brown sugar

1 teaspoon (6 g) kosher or sea salt

4 salmon fillets, each about 6 ounces (168 g)

2 tablespoons (28 g) alder wood chips

2 tablespoons (28 ml) olive oil

2 thick slices pancetta (about 2 ounces [55 g]), diced

2 shallots, diced

1 cup (130 g) frozen green peas, thawed, drained

1½ cups (355 ml) dry white wine

3 tablespoons (42 g) cold butter, cut into chunks

⅔ cup (157 ml) heavy cream

Salt and fresh cracked black pepper to taste

1 teaspoon (2 g) minced fresh chives

1 teaspoon (2 g) freshly chopped Italian flat-leaf parsley

Bring large stock of pot of salted water to boil, then cook pasta until al dente, about 9 minutes. Drain, rinse in cold water, and set aside. Place small skillet over medium-high heat, add cumin and fennel seeds and toast, tossing in pan for 3 minutes or until aromatic. Transfer toasted seeds to spice grinder or a mortar and grind until coarse. Transfer to bowl and combine with brown sugar, black pepper, and salt. Rub each salmon fillet, skin side down, with spice rub. Prepare stovetop smoker with wood chips in bottom. Place salmon on rack, cover with lid, and smoke over medium heat for 45 minutes. Remove from heat and let stand, uncovered for 10 minutes.

Heat olive oil in large skillet over medium-high heat, add pancetta and cook, stirring occasionally, until crisp and fat is rendered. Remove pancetta and set aside. Add shallot to skillet and sauté until tender, about 3 minutes. Add white wine to deglaze skillet, scraping brown bits off bottom and sides of skillet. Reduce wine by one third, then add peas and heavy cream and stir to heat through. Bring sauce to boil and cook for 3 minutes. Gradually stir in butter, then let sauce reduce and thicken for about 5 minutes. Season with salt and black pepper. Remove salmon from smoker and serve with pasta and sauce. Garnish with chopped chives, parsley, and crumbled pancetta.

Rosemary Smoked **Shrimp Kabobs with Shallot-Apricot Glaze**

Rosemary is a robust herb that adds tremendous flavor to any grilled dish. To some it may seem a bit overpowering, but it is a special flavor that, when used the right way, adds just the right touch. Rosemary skewers, long sticks of fresh rosemary stripped of their leaves, serve as a great utensil for flavoring these grilled shrimp.

4 rosemary skewers (substitute wooden or metal skewers if desired)

24 large shrimp, peeled and deveined, but tails left intact

24 large button mushrooms

16 cloves garlic, peeled

1/2 cup (50 g) Spicy Dry Rub (see recipe page 24)

1/4 cup (60 ml) olive oil

2 tablespoons (28 g) alder wood chips

2 tablespoons (28 g) butter

1/4 cup (40 g) chopped fresh shallots

1/2 (160 g) cup apricot preserves

2 tablespoons (28 ml) brandy

1 tablespoon (9 g) dry mustard

1 teaspoon (5 ml) white balsamic vinegar

1/2 teaspoon (1 g) cinnamon

Juice of one lemon

If using rosemary skewers, strip most of the leaves, but leave about 2 inches (5 cm) intact at top. Working in separate bowls for each ingredient, rub shrimp, mushrooms, and garlic with dry rub. Thread 3 shrimp, 3 mushrooms, and 2 garlic cloves on each skewer, starting with shrimp and ending with mushrooms, and alternating each item.

Place alder wood chips in bottom of smoker, add drip pan and smoking rack to smoker, and spray rack with nonstick cooking spray. Place kabobs on rack, cover, and smoke over medium heat for 30 minutes.

Remove from heat and let stand 5 minutes. Melt butter in small saucepan over medium-high heat, then add shallots and cook until tender, about 4 minutes. Add apricot preserves and bring to slow boil, then add brandy and cook for 2 minutes, or until bubbles subside. Add dry mustard, balsamic vinegar, cinnamon, and lemon juice and stir to combine. Remove kabobs from smoker and serve topped with Shallot-Apricot Glaze.

Grill-**Seared Tuna with Mango-Wasabi Relish**

With the sushi craze in full bloom, tuna and wasabi are rarely thought of separately. The hot fire of wasabi pairs beautifully here with the sweet, cooling bite of mango on top of these juicy seared tuna steaks.

4 Ahi tuna steaks, at least 1" (2.5 cm) thick

FOR THE MARINADE:

1 cup (235 ml) soy sauce

1 tablespoon (6 g) minced fresh ginger

1 tablespoon (10 g) minced fresh garlic

2 scallions, sliced thin

⅓ cup (39 g) sugar

⅓ cup (78 ml) sake

½ teaspoon (1 g) red pepperflakes

1 tablespoon (14 ml) vegetable oil

1 large carrot, sliced julienne

1 red onion, sliced julienne

½ cup (25 g) bean sprouts

1½ English cucumber, deseeded and sliced julienne

½ tablespoon (11 g) toasted white sesame seeds

½ tablespoon (11 g) black sesame seeds

Juice of one lemon

FOR MANGO-WASABI RELISH:

3 cups (450 g) chopped mango (about 3 large mangos)

½ cup (30 g) chopped fresh mint

½ cup (30 g) chopped fresh cilantro

1 jalapeño chile, seeded and finely chopped

1 scallion, sliced thin

1 tablespoon (14 ml) rice vinegar

Juice of 2 limes

1 tablespoon (14 ml) soy sauce

½ teaspoon (3 g) wasabi paste

1 tablespoon (14 ml) sesame oil

2 tablespoons (28 ml) peanut oil

Combine marinade ingredients in large bowl, then cover and marinate tuna for at least 1 hour in refrigerator. For the relish, combine mango, mint, cilantro, chile, and scallion. Combine rice vinegar with lime juice, soy sauce, and wasabi paste in medium mixing bowl, then gradually add oil, whisking to combine. Add wasabi mixture to mango mixture, season with salt and pepper, stir to combine, cover, and refrigerate for at least 1 hour.

Heat vegetable oil in sauté pan over medium-high heat. Add carrot and onion and sauté until just tender, about 3 minutes. Add sprouts, toss together just to wilt, and transfer mixture to a serving bowl. Add cucumber, sesame seeds, and lemon juice, toss to combine, season with salt and pepper, and set aside. Spray stovetop grill pan with nonstick cooking spray. Preheat grill pan to high heat. Remove tuna from marinade and place on hot grill, searing each side quickly, about 3 minutes per side. Remove, slice thinly, and serve over sautéed vegetables with Mango-Wasabi Relish on top.

chapter 7

Vegetables

Smoked **Corn on the Cob**

This may be the easiest recipe in the book, but it's also one of the most flavorful. Smoked corn makes a tremendous side dish for most of the grilled or smoked meals in this book. Alternatively, serve the corn as a complement to a salad, cut from the cob, or inside a grilled quesadilla.

4 ears fresh corn

1 tablespoon (9 g) chili powder

½ teaspoon (1 g) paprika

½ teaspoon (1 g) garlic salt

½ teaspoon (1 g) coarse ground black pepper

Nonstick vegetable spray

1 teaspoon (5 g) corncob wood chips

1 tablespoon (14 g) apple wood chips

Combine chili powder, paprika, garlic salt, and pepper in small mixing bowl and stir to combine. Pull back husk on each ear of corn, keeping husk intact, and remove silk on inside of corn. Spray corn evenly with cooking spray and sprinkle each cob evenly with spice mixture. Gather husks up around corn, closing in spices. Combine wood chips and place in bottom of stovetop smoker, then top with smoking rack. Place corn on smoking rack and close lid tight. Place smoker on a burner over medium heat. Smoke corn for 20 minutes. Remove from heat without removing lid and continue smoking for 15 additional minutes. Remove lid, pull back husks, and serve hot.

Smoked **Sweet Potato Mash**

Sweet potatoes are a great mashing potato. With wonderful natural sugars, the combination of smoked flavors and natural sweetness are a perfect match.

6 medium-sized sweet potatoes, scrubbed

1 tablespoon (14 g) apple wood chips

1 tablespoon (14 g) pecan wood chips

3 tablespoons (42 g) butter

2 tablespoons (28 ml) heavy cream

3 tablespoons (60 g) honey

2 tablespoons (28 g) brown sugar

$\frac{1}{2}$ teaspoon (1 g) ground nutmeg

$\frac{1}{2}$ teaspoon (3 g) salt

$\frac{1}{2}$ teaspoon (1 g) freshly cracked black pepper

8 ounces (225 g) miniature marshmallows

$\frac{1}{3}$ cup (42 g) chopped pecans, toasted

Place unpeeled sweet potatoes in saucepan, bring to boil, cover, and boil for 20 minutes. Remove and drain, then cut in half lengthwise. Position wood chips in bottom of stovetop smoker. Place potatoes on smoking rack and smoke over medium heat for 20 minutes. Remove from smoker and place in large mixing bowl. When cool enough to handle, remove skins and discard. Add butter, heavy cream, honey, brown sugar, nutmeg, salt, and pepper to bowl. Using a potato masher, mash potatoes to combine all ingredients. Place potatoes in casserole dish, top with marshmallows and pecans, place on center rack of oven under broiler, and toast for about 3 minutes or until marshmallows are melted and beginning to brown. (Browning time will vary from oven to oven; watch the marshmallows closely.) Turn oven to 375°F (190°C) and bake potatoes for 15 minutes or until warmed through. (Cover with lid or aluminum foil if needed to prevent marshmallows from burning.) Serve warm.

[Makes 4 Servings]

Grilled **Vegetable Quesadillas**

Quesadillas are a very simple way to cook an entire meal in a short period of time, and they pack a lot of flavor into one item. Using an indoor grill makes the preparation easy and adds attractive grill marks on the folded flour tortillas. For this recipe, I use traditional flour tortillas, but you can substitute any flavor and size of wrap or tortilla.

1 large yellow squash, cut into ¼" (5 mm)-thick diagonal slices

1 large green zucchini, cut into ¼" (5 mm)-thick diagonal slices

1 cup thinly sliced shitake mushrooms, stems removed

1 cup thinly sliced oyster mushrooms, woody stems removed

8 green onions, chopped

2 tablespoons (28 ml) vegetable oil

Salt

Black pepper

4 large (burrito size) flour tortillas or other wraps

2 tablespoons (28 g) butter, softened (or vegetable oil cooking spray)

1½ cups (170 g) shredded Monterey Jack cheese

1 cup (113 g) shredded smoked Gouda cheese

½ cup (115 g) Cilantro-Infused Sour Cream (recipe follows)

FOR CILANTRO-INFUSED SOUR CREAM:

1 bunch cilantro leaves picked from the stems

1 tablespoon (14 ml) olive oil

1 tablespoon (14 ml) fresh lime juice

1 teaspoon (3 g) ground cumin

½ teaspoon (3 g) salt

½ teaspoon (1 g) fresh cracked black pepper

½ cup (115 g) sour cream

[For Infused Sour Cream]
In bowl of food processor fitted with blade attachment, pulse cilantro leaves with oil and lime juice just until chopped. Add cumin, season with salt and pepper, and pulse to purée. Transfer cilantro mix to bowl, add sour cream, and stir to combiner. Season with salt and pepper, if desired, then cover and chill before serving. May be made ahead of time and refrigerated for up to one week.

[For the Quesadillas]
Preheat stovetop grill pan on burner set to high heat, or preheat an electric grill to high. Toss sliced zucchini, squash, mushrooms, and green onion with vegetable oil and season with salt and pepper. If using stovetop grill pan, grill squash and zucchini first, about 4 to 5 minutes per side, or just until tender and brown. Then grill mushrooms and green onion, turning and tossing to grill evenly, about 5 to 7 minutes total grilling time.

If using electric grill, cook as many items at same time as will fit onto grill. Note: mushrooms grill faster, though not as evenly as larger items, so turn and toss as necessary. Regardless of method, grill vegetables until dark grill marks appear and vegetables are tender. Remove vegetables and set aside to cool.

Combine grated cheeses in small bowl and set aside. Working with all ingredients at hand, place tortillas on flat work surface and divide ingredients equally among quesadillas. Set aside about ½ cup (57 g) of shredded cheese and then divide rest, placing one quarter of the cheese on half of each tortilla. Top cheese with grilled vegetables, dividing evenly among tortillas, then season to taste and sprinkle each with remaining cheese. Fold each tortilla in half, spread topmost outer surface with butter, place on grill, buttered side down, and spread top with butter. If using electric grill, close lid and grill for about 7 minutes or until brown and cheese is melted. If using stovetop grill pan, grill each side until brown and cheese is melted about 6 minutes per side. Place quesadillas on cutting board, let stand for 3 minutes, then cut each into wedges, drizzle with Cilantro-Infused Sour Cream, and serve.

[Makes 16 skewers (8 servings)]

Grilled **Vegetable Kabobs with Honey-Balsamic Glaze**

Grilling vegetables is one of the best ways to enjoy garden-fresh produce. Even indoor grilling brings out the tremendous flavor of fresh vegetables, enhancing them with a robust, earthy elegance. For this recipe, I recommend using an open grilling appliance versus a closed panini grill because you want the vegetables to cook fast, which sears in their natural juices and flavors while keeping them tender but firm. You will also need sixteen 10-inch (25 cm) bamboo or metal skewers.

2 red peppers, cut into 1¹/₂"
(4 cm) pieces

2 green peppers, cut into
1¹/₂" (4 cm) pieces

2 yellow peppers, cut into
1¹/₂" (4 cm) pieces

4 yellow onions, cut into 1¹/₂"
(4 cm) pieces

2 large yellow squash, cut into
1¹/₂" (4 cm) pieces

2 large zucchini, cut into 1¹/₂"
(4 cm) pieces

1 medium eggplant, cut into 1¹/₂"
(4 cm) pieces

32 small button or crimini
mushrooms, wiped clean and
stems trimmed

¹/₄ cup (60 ml) olive oil

Kosher salt

Fresh ground black pepper

1 teaspoon (1 g) garlic powder

1 teaspoon (1 g) chili powder

FOR HONEY-BALSAMIC GLAZE:

1 tablespoon (14 ml) olive oil

1 tablespoon (14 g) butter

1 shallot, finely chopped

1 clove fresh garlic (about
1 tablespoon [10 g]), finely minced

1 cup (235 ml) apple cider

2 large pieces of orange rind,
white pith removed

3 tablespoons (42 ml) balsamic
vinegar

1 tablespoon (20 g) honey

Salt and fresh ground black
pepper to taste

The balsamic glaze that accompanies this recipe works well with other grilled dishes such as meat, chicken, and fish.

If using bamboo or wooden skewers, soak in water, fully submerged, for about 2 hours to prevent them from burning on the grill. Working in batches, thread vegetables, alternating among them, onto skewers. Combine salt, pepper, garlic powder, and chili powder in small bowl, then dust all skewers evenly with spice mixture and set aside.

If using stovetop grill pan, spray with nonstick cooking spray. Preheat electric grill or stovetop grill pan to high heat.

Grill kabobs in batches for about 15 minutes, turning a few times, until brown and tender. Remove from grill and set aside in warm oven until ready to serve.

To make glaze, melt butter with olive oil in small saucepan over medium heat. Add shallots and garlic and sauté until tender, about 4 minutes. Add apple cider and orange rind, bring to a boil, and reduce to about ½ cup (120 ml), which will take about 20 minutes. Add balsamic vinegar and honey, stir to combine, and cook for about 3 minutes to thicken. Season with salt and pepper and serve alongside hot vegetable kabobs.

3 tablespoons (42 ml) peanut oil

2 tablespoons (26 g) sugar

4 tablespoons (60 ml) rice vinegar

4 tablespoons (60 ml) soy sauce

2 teaspoons (12 g) minced ginger

2 teaspoons (10 ml) hot chili sauce

2 (16 ounce [455 g]) packages extra-firm tofu, drained

2 cups (390 g) jasmine rice

4 cups (950 ml) water

2 teaspoons (10 ml) dark sesame oil

1½ pounds (680 g) grilled asparagus, chopped

1 pound (455 g) baby bok choy, grilled and thinly sliced

1¼ cups (163 g) julienne carrot

2 teaspoons (12 g) salt

½ teaspoon (1 g) black pepper

2 tablespoons (28 g) wood chips

Nonstick cooking spray

Marinated Smoked **Tofu** over Asparagus and Jasmine Rice

Jasmine rice adds beautiful flavor to any meal, and the texture and smoked subtleties of the tofu in this recipe makes a perfect pairing. Tofu comes in several different textures; for this recipe, I recommend using extra-firm tofu so it will stand up to grilling. Be sure you drain the liquid off any tofu before marinating and smoking.

For the marinade, combine 2 tablespoons (28 ml) peanut oil, sugar, rice vinegar, soy sauce, minced ginger, and chili sauce in large bowl and whisk to combine.

Place wood chips in bottom of smoker and spray bottom rack and smoking rack with nonstick cooking spray.

Place tofu in shallow dish, pour marinade over to coat, reserving ½ cup (120 ml) for later use. Cover and refrigerate at least 1 hour. Remove tofu from refrigerator and place on cooling rack set on sheet pan to drain, about 5 minutes. Place tofu in smoker, close lid, and smoke for 20 minutes. Let cool. When cool enough to handle, cut into 1" (2.5 cm) cubes.

Combine rice and water in 2-quart saucepan and bring to boil over high heat. Stir rice to loosen, reduce heat to low simmer, cover, and cook for 20 minutes, stirring occasionally, until rice is tender and all moisture is absorbed. Once cooked, remove pan from heat and set aside.

Grill asparagus and bok choy following method described on page 112. Remove from grill and set aside.

In large wok or skillet, heat remaining 1 tablespoon (14 ml) of peanut oil with sesame oil over medium-high heat. Add tofu, grilled asparagus, bok choy, and carrots. Toss to heat through, then pour in reserved marinade, toss again, and season with salt and black pepper. Serve hot over jasmine rice.

Grilled **Eggplant Roulades with Smoked Tomato Sauce**

Eggplant can be prepared in many ways, making it a versatile vegetarian meal. In this recipe, the eggplant is stuffed and rolled with ricotta cheese before grilling. To serve, top with smoky tomato sauce.

3 large eggplants, sliced into
1/4" (5 mm)-thick slices lengthwise

12 slices prosciutto, thinly sliced

1 cup (250 g) ricotta cheese

1/2 cup (120 g) marscapone cheese
(room temperature)

1/4 cup (25 g) grated parmigiano-
reggiano cheese

1/4 cup (28 g) shredded
mozzarella cheese

1/4 cup (15 g) packed fresh
basil, chopped

2 ounces (13 g) sun-dried
tomatoes, chopped

4 ounces (50 g) pitted kalamata
olives, chopped

2 ounces (25 g) pitted Greek
green olives, chopped

2 anchovy fillets, packed in oil
and salt

1 teaspoon (1 g) fresh
oregano, minced

1 tablespoon (15 g) capers

1 tablespoon (20 g) honey

1 tablespoon (28 ml) balsamic
vinegar

Salt and black pepper to taste

2 cups (500 g) Smoked Tomato
Sauce (see recipe page 42)

1/4 cup (60 ml) olive oil, divided

1 tablespoon (14 g) butter

1/4 cup (60 ml) Madeira or sherry

Preheat stovetop grill pan or electric grill to medium-high heat. Brush both sides of eggplant with olive oil, and season with salt and pepper. Grill eggplant on both sides until brown, about 6 minutes per side in grill pan and 7 minutes total on grill press. Remove and set aside to cool. Preheat oven to 350°F (180°C).

Combine ricotta cheese with mascarpone, parmigiano-reggiano, mozzarella, and basil in mixing bowl. Mix with fork until thoroughly combined, then cover and refrigerate for at least 30 minutes. Combine sun-dried tomatoes with both types of olives, anchovy filets, oregano, capers, honey, and balsamic vinegar in food processor fitted with blade attachment. Pulse to chop into coarse mixture, then season with salt and black pepper.

Working on flat surface, lay grilled eggplant slices in row. Layer each slice with prosciut to and top with spoonful of ricotta cheese mixture. Roll eggplant into roulade. Coat bottom of 9" × 13" (23 × 33 cm) baking dish evenly with 1 cup (250 g) smoked tomato sauce. Place eggplant roulades in baking dish and drizzle with remaining smoked tomato sauce. Bake until cheese is melted, about 20 minutes.

Meanwhile, heat 2 tablespoons (28 ml) olive oil in skillet over medium heat. Add olive tapenade mixture to skillet and heat through, about 5 minutes. Deglaze pan with Madeira, reduce by half, then add butter and stir to combine. Remove roulades from oven, serve, and top with olive tapenade.

chapter 8

Sweet Endings

Panini-Grilled S'more Sandwiches with Chocolate Fondue

If your child is in the Boy or Girl Scouts or you do any kind of camping or outdoor grilling, you probably know all about s'mores (as in have *some more*) and how great they are. I decided to develop a recipe that brings all the goodness of outdoor toasted marshmallows indoors. Panini Grilled S'more Sandwiches are a triumph of indoor grilling.

¾ cup (175 ml) heavy cream

1 cinnamon stick

6 ounces (168 g) semisweet chocolate, chopped (or chips)

8 thick slices cinnamon swirl bread

3 tablespoons (42 g) butter, softened

1 cup (260 g) chunky peanut butter

1 large, ripe banana, cut in half then sliced into thin slices lengthwise

1 cup (225 g) Marshmallow Fluff

For the chocolate fondue, heat heavy cream with cinnamon stick in small nonstick saucepan over medium heat just until steaming. Add chocolate and stir aggressively to incorporate and melt. Remove from heat and set aside, stirring occasionally to incorporate chocolate.

Preheat panini grill to high heat. Working with four slices of bread, spread peanut butter evenly on one side, dividing equally among four slices. Spread marshmallow on other four slices of bread, again dividing equally among slices. Place sliced bananas in single layer on top of peanut butter, dividing evenly among sandwiches. Pair the sandwiches up, closing peanut butter and fluff sides together. Butter top of sandwiches and place buttered side down on hot grill. Spread butter on remaining side and close grill. Cook for 7 minutes, or until toasted and marshmallow begins to melt. Remove, let cool for 5 minutes, cut in half diagonally, and serve drizzled with chocolate fondue.

Grilled **Strawberry Parfait**

You can always make a parfait with fresh strawberries, so why grill them at all? The answer: grilling the strawberries intensifies their flavors and caramelizes their natural sugars in the process. Be gentle when grilling strawberries, however, as they are delicate. First, choose large, firm berries and then grill them only until marked with grill marks and just tender to the touch; overgrilling will turn them to mush. This recipe can be used with a variety of fruits, including peaches, apricots, and assorted fresh berries.

1 pint (220 g) large strawberries

⅓ cup (78 ml) amaretto liqueur, plus 2 tablespoons (28 ml)

FOR THE WHIPPED CREAM:

3 cups (690 g) heavy cream

2 teaspoons (10 ml) vanilla extract

¼ cup (25 g) confectioners' sugar

12 ginger snap cookies

¼ cup (70 g) melted vanilla ice cream

Shaved chocolate for garnish

4 sprigs fresh mint for garnish

This recipe uses melted vanilla ice cream instead of Crème Anglaise, the more traditional dessert topping. This will save you time and fuss in the kitchen. When selecting ice cream, choose a good-quality brand for the best results.

Cut strawberries in half lengthwise, setting aside four whole berries for garnish. If using stovetop grill pan, spray with nonstick cooking spray. Preheat stovetop grill pan or electric grill to high heat. Place strawberries on grill, seeded side facing up, and grill for 4 minutes. Turn and grill for 4 additional minutes, or until tender. Remove and set aside to cool. When cool, toss strawberries with honey and liqueur, then cover and refrigerate for at least 1 hour to macerate.

Using electric mixer and large bowl, whisk cream to soft peaks. Add vanilla and confectioners' sugar and whip to form stiff peaks. Set aside. Place ginger snaps in bowl of a food processor fitted with blade attachment, process until reaching fine crumbled consistency, and set aside. Cut the pound cake into four 1" (2.5 cm)-thick slices and then into 1" (2.5 cm) cubes. Set aside.

To make parfait, use cocktail or champagne glasses. Begin layering pound cake in bottom drizzled with 1 teaspoon (5 ml) liqueur and then 1 teaspoon (5 ml) melted vanilla ice cream. Top with 1 teaspoon (5 g) ground ginger snap cookies and then one spoonful of strawberries. Top strawberries with large spoonful of whipped cream. Repeat process to fill glass. Garnish with shaved chocolate and fresh mint. Serve immediately or cover with plastic wrap and refrigerate for only up to 2 hours. (If making parfaits ahead of time, stop layering after last addition of strawberries and save final whipped cream and ginger snaps until just before serving.)

Grilled **Bananas Foster with Vanilla Bean Ice Cream**

Bananas Foster is a classic dessert packed with intense flavor. Grilling the bananas gives them visual appeal as well as a wonderful caramelized flavor. Note: I do not recommend using a grill with a closing lid for this recipe, as bananas are tender, and the lid would likely flatten them.

3 ripe bananas, peeled, cut in half vertically, and then cut in half horizontally

1 stick (½ cup [55 g]) butter

⅓ cup (75 g) brown sugar

1 teaspoon (3 g) cinnamon

⅓ cup (78 ml) brandy

¼ cup (60 ml) banana liqueur

1 pint (285 g) favorite vanilla ice cream

1 cup (235 ml) whipped cream

Brush stovetop grill pan evenly with vegetable oil by drizzling oil over pan and then wiping with paper towel (be sure to cover entire surface thoroughly). Preheat grill pan to medium-high heat.

Spray banana slices with nonstick cooking spray and position, flat side down, on grill pan. Grill until black grill marks appear and banana just becomes tender, about 6 minutes. Turn and continue grilling for an additional 5 minutes. Do not allow banana to become overly tender or mushy. Remove bananas and set aside.

In large, nonstick sauté pan, melt butter over medium heat. Add brown sugar and cinnamon, then stir to combine. Add grilled banana slices to pan in one even layer. Using spoon, dip into sauce and pour gently over bananas to coat evenly. Cook for 3 minutes, then add brandy and banana liqueur to pan. Swirl to combine, then cook for additional 3 minutes to allow alcohol to cook off. Place scoops of vanilla ice cream into serving bowls, add banana slices and sauce, then top with whipped cream and serve.

Grilled **Pears over Rice Pudding**

One of my favorite homemade desserts is a rich and creamy rice pudding. This dish pairs a favorite recipe from my childhood with grilled pears and almond lace cookies.

4 red or Anjou pears, cored

3 cups (705 ml) apple cider

1 cup (235 ml) orange juice

1 cup (235 ml) ruby port

2 cinnamon sticks

2 whole cloves

FOR THE RICE PUDDING:

1/2 cup (75 g) golden raisins

1/4 cup (60 ml) dark rum

2 3/4 cups (645 ml) whole milk

1 cup (185 g) basmati or long grain white rice

1/2 cup (113 g) firmly packed light brown sugar

1/2 cup (100 g) granulated sugar

2 tablespoons (28 g) unsalted butter

1 teaspoon (6 g) salt

1/4 (0.5 g) teaspoon ground cinnamon

1 cup (235 ml) half-and-half, plus 3/4 cup (175 ml)

1 tablespoon (8 g) cornstarch

3 large egg yolks, lightly beaten

1 1/2 teaspoons (7.5 ml) vanilla extract

8 Almond Lace Cookies (recipe follows)

Combine apple cider, orange juice, port, cinnamon sticks, and cloves in large stockpot and bring to boil over high heat. Place pears in boiling liquid and cook for 20 minutes or until tender. Remove, drain, and set aside to cool.

Meanwhile, combine raisins and rum in small nonstick saucepan and bring to boil over medium-high heat. Remove pan from heat and let raisins steep. Combine milk, rice, brown sugar, granulated sugar, butter, salt, cinnamon, and 1 cup (235 ml) of half-and-half in medium-size heavy saucepan. Cook over medium heat until mixture comes to gentle boil, stir, cover, and reduce heat to low. Cook for 40 to 45 minutes or until rice is cooked through and most of liquid is absorbed.

Place cornstarch in small bowl, then gradually whisk in remaining half-and-half until smooth. Add egg yolks and whisk until smooth. Whisk about 1/2 cup (80 g) of hot rice mixture into yolk mixture. Return new mixture to pudding in saucepan. Cook over medium heat, stirring constantly, until mixture just starts to bubble. Continue to cook, stirring, for 1 more minute, or until mixture thickens slightly. Remove the pan from the heat. Add vanilla to rum raisin mixture, then stir mixture into rice pudding. Transfer pudding to large baking dish and spread into

shallow layer. Cover completely with plastic wrap, pressing plastic directly onto top of pudding, and refrigerate for at least 2 hours or until well chilled.

Before serving, spray a stovetop grill pan with nonstick cooking spray and preheat to high heat or preheat electric grill to high heat. Cut each pear in half, place flesh side down, and grill for 7 minutes or until brown and caramelized. Remove and serve in an almond cookie topped with rice pudding.

FOR ALMOND LACE COOKIES:

3/4 cup (150 g) sugar

4 1/2 tablespoons (62 g) unsalted butter

3 tablespoons (60 g) honey

4 1/2 tablespoons (67 ml) heavy cream

1/4 teaspoon (1.2 ml) almond extract

3 tablespoons (72 g) all-purpose flour

1 cup (125 g) sliced almonds

Preheat oven to 400°F (200°C). Combine sugar, butter, honey, and cream in small heavy saucepan and bring to boil over medium heat, stirring constantly, for about 3 minutes. Remove pan from heat, stir in almond extract, flour, and almonds, then let mixture cool for 3 minutes. (The mixture will thicken and harden as it cools.)

Spoon rounded scoops (about the size of golf balls) onto baking sheets lined with parchment paper; scoops should be about

4" (10 cm) apart. Bake on middle rack of oven for 5 to 8 minutes or until cookies are golden brown. Slide parchment paper with the cookies onto cooling rack and let cool for 1 minute. Using a spatula, pick cookies off paper and drape over bottom of large measuring cup or small bowl to form cup shapes. Work quickly to shape cups, as the cookies cool quickly and become brittle as they cool. If this happens, break cookies into large pieces to use as garnish.

Index

Acknowledgments

When the idea for an indoor grilling and smoking book was presented to me, I immediately thought it was a great idea. Visit any store and you're sure to find some type of indoor grilling appliance. In fact, I had been given an indoor smoker as a gift a few years back, but had never used it. This project forced me to take it out of the box and, sure enough, over time, I fell in love with an entirely new way of cooking. I hope these pages will inspire you to explore and create in the kitchen.

It isn't without tremendous input from many very talented people that a book comes together. I have, once again, been very lucky to be surrounded by tremendous talent and grace. I thank everyone at Rockport Publishers for the opportunity to translate my thoughts and ideas into a very beautiful piece of work. To Winnie Prentiss, Publisher; Delilah Smittle, Editor; and Rosalind Wanke, Art Director—I thank each of you individually for your perseverance and patience throughout the project. Without them, my work would only be pages of scribble. Thank you also to Allan Penn, the book's photographer, for turning my food into beautiful artwork. Allan is tremendously encouraging on our photo shoots and I trust and value his work; he is a truly talented, gifted friend.

I also want to thank all my family and friends who continuously encourage and inspire me. To Tony, Randy, Steve and Erin, Kerri and Bryan, Cliff and Kathy, Theresa and Joe —thank you all collectively for always having my best interest at heart, and yes, for your discriminating taste buds. Special thanks also to Tony for his patience as I constantly mess up the kitchen.

And, as always, thank you to all the readers who choose my books over others to inspire their cooking endeavors. I hope that with *Indoor Grilling* I have, once again, provided a mouthwatering collection of simple recipes that not only give you guidance in the kitchen but also inspire your own creativity. Enjoy!

About the Author

Dwayne Ridgaway, a native of Kerrville, Texas, currently resides in Bristol, Rhode Island. He is the author of the well-received *Lasagna: The Art of Layered Cooking; Pizza: 50 Traditional and Alternative Recipes for the Oven and Grill;* and *Sandwiches, Panini, and Wraps: Recipes for the Original "Anytime, Anywhere" Meal* and a contributing author, food stylist, and recipe developer for several notable magazines and books. Dwayne, a graduate of the highly respected Johnson and Wales University, currently works in Rhode Island as a food and beverage consultant, caterer, and event designer. He has, in short, made a career out of exploring and celebrating the culinary arts. His passions lie in fresh ingredients and new flavors, giving him the ability to develop new and exciting recipes that any reader can execute and enjoy. Dwayne's goal is for all readers to use his recipes and writing as a groundwork for their own personal creativity.